SHURLEY ENGLISH

English Made Easy

This booklet belongs to:

Student Workbook   Level 3

SHURLEY INSTRUCTIONAL MATERIALS, INC., CABOT, ARKANSAS

01-09
ISBN 978-1-58561-107-2 (Level 3 Student Workbook)

For additional information or to place an order, write to: Shurley Instructional Materials, Inc.
366 SIM Drive
Cabot, AR 72023

1 2   09 07

Study Skills Assessment

Directions: Rate your skills in each category by marking the appropriate column with an **X**.

GET ORGANIZED: Reference 2	Excellent	Average	Needs Improvement
1. Being prepared.	☐	☐	☐
2. Organizing your desk	☐	☐	☐
3. Putting everything in its place.	☐	☐	☐
4. Realizing the importance of directions	☐	☐	☐
5. Proofreading your work	☐	☐	☐

LISTEN: Reference 3	Excellent	Average	Needs Improvement
1. Listening with your whole body	☐	☐	☐
2. Asking questions	☐	☐	☐
3. Taking notes	☐	☐	☐
4. Concentrating	☐	☐	☐
5. Listening to directions	☐	☐	☐

PLAN YOUR TIME: Reference 4	Excellent	Average	Needs Improvement
1. Setting goals for yourself	☐	☐	☐
2. Planning your day	☐	☐	☐
3. Doing what is important first	☐	☐	☐
4. Making each minute count.	☐	☐	☐
5. Rewarding yourself.	☐	☐	☐

DO YOUR HOMEWORK: Reference 5	Excellent	Average	Needs Improvement
1. Collecting assignments before you leave school	☐	☐	☐
2. Scheduling a time to study.	☐	☐	☐
3. Studying where you can concentrate	☐	☐	☐
4. Setting a time limit to study.	☐	☐	☐
5. Having a special place to keep homework	☐	☐	☐

If you marked any areas as "Average" or "Needs Improvement," look back at the references in those areas to help you find ways to improve. Find a study-skills partner to check your progress, to encourage you, and to give you advice and help.

Notes: _____

_____

_____

_____

_____

_____

_____

_____

_____

_____

_____

_____

_____

_____

_____

_____

_____

_____

_____

_____

_____

_____

_____

_____

_____

_____

_____

_____

_____

Classroom Practice 1

Name:_____ Date:_____

SKILLS

▶ **Exercise 1:** Using Reference 11 on pages 13–14, write the correct rule number beside each **capitalization** rule.

_____ 1. Capitalize the names and nicknames of people.

_____ 2. Capitalize titles used with, or in place of, people's names.

_____ 3. Capitalize the days of the week and months of the year.

_____ 4. Capitalize family names when used in place of or with the person's name.

_____ 5. Capitalize the names and abbreviations of cities, towns, counties, states, and countries.

_____ 6. Capitalize the pronoun I.

_____ 7. Capitalize the first word of a sentence.

_____ 8. Capitalize the names of avenues, streets, roads, highways, routes, and post office boxes.

_____ 9. Capitalize the names of pets.

_____ 10. Capitalize the names of holidays.

_____ 11. Capitalize people's initials.

EDITING

▶ **Exercise 2:** Write the capitalization rule numbers for each correction in **bold**.
Use Reference 11 on pages 13–14 to look up the capitalization rule numbers.

I saw a painting of Captain James Cook in an art gallery in London, England.

▶ **Exercise 3:** Find each capitalization mistake and write the correction above it.

madison square garden is an indoor sports arena in new york city, new york.

SHURLEY ENGLISH

Notes:
_____
_____
_____
_____
_____
_____
_____
_____
_____
_____
_____
_____
_____
_____
_____
_____
_____
_____
_____
_____
_____
_____
_____
_____
_____
_____
_____
_____
_____

Classroom Practice 2

Name:_____ Date:_____

SKILLS

▶ **Exercise 1:** Using References 13–14 on pages 17–19, write the correct rule number beside each **punctuation** rule.

_____ 1. Use a period after most abbreviations or titles that are accepted in formal writing.

_____ 2. Use a comma to separate words or phrases in a series.

_____ 3. Use a comma between the day of the week and the month and day. Use a comma between the day and year.

_____ 4. Use a comma to separate the city from the state.

_____ 5. Use a question mark for the end punctuation of a sentence that asks a question.

_____ 6. Use a period after initials.

_____ 7. Use underlining or italics for titles of books, magazines, works of art, ships, and newspapers.

_____ 8. Use commas to separate a noun of direct address from the rest of the sentence.

▶ **Exercise 2:** Using Reference 11 on pages 13–14, write the correct rule number beside each **capitalization** rule.

_____ 1. Capitalize titles used with, or in place of, people's names.

_____ 2. Capitalize the days of the week and months of the year.

_____ 3. Capitalize proper adjectives.

_____ 4. Capitalize family names when used in place of or with the person's name.

_____ 5. Capitalize the names and abbreviations of cities, towns, counties, states, and countries.

_____ 6. Capitalize the pronoun I.

_____ 7. Capitalize the names of avenues, streets, roads, highways, routes, and post office boxes.

_____ 8. Capitalize people's initials.

EDITING

▶ **Exercise 3:** Write the capitalization and punctuation rule numbers for each correction in **bold**. Use References 11, 13, and 14 on pages 13–14 and 17–19 to look up the capitalization and punctuation rule numbers.

Did **Mr.** James Lewis move to Crestwood, Maryland, on Sunday, September 4, 2007**?**

▶ **Exercise 4:** Put punctuation corrections within the sentence. Write all other corrections above the sentence.
Editing Guide: Capitals: 6   Commas: 3   Apostrophes: 1   End Marks: 1

yes tony roger and hank came to justins birthday party on friday

Notes: _____

_____

_____

_____

_____

_____

_____

_____

_____

_____

_____

_____

_____

_____

_____

_____

_____

_____

_____

_____

_____

_____

_____

_____

_____

_____

_____

_____

Classroom Practice 3

Name:_____ Date:_____

SKILLS

▶ **Exercise 1:** Match the definitions by writing the correct letter beside each number.

_____ 1. periods, commas, apostrophes, end marks   A. synonyms

_____ 2. words with similar meanings   B. antonyms

_____ 3. words with opposite meanings   C. punctuation

▶ **Exercise 2:** Identify each pair of words as synonyms or antonyms by underlining the correct answer.

1. arrive, leave   2. harm, injure   3. smile, frown

Synonyms or Antonyms   Synonyms or Antonyms   Synonyms or Antonyms

▶ **Exercise 3:** Using References 13–14 on pages 17–19, write the correct rule number beside each **punctuation** rule.

_____ 1. Use a comma to separate words or phrases in a series.

_____ 2. Use a comma between the day of the week and the month and day. Use a comma between the day and year.

_____ 3. Use a comma to separate the city from the state.

_____ 4. Use a period after initials.

_____ 5. Use a comma after the year when the complete date is used in the middle of the sentence.

_____ 6. Use commas to separate a noun of direct address from the rest of the sentence.

▶ **Exercise 4:** Using Reference 11 on pages 13–14, write the correct rule number beside each **capitalization** rule.

_____ 1. Capitalize titles used with, or in place of, people's names.

_____ 2. Capitalize family names when used in place of or with the person's name.

_____ 3. Capitalize the names of avenues, streets, roads, highways, routes, and post office boxes.

_____ 4. Capitalize people's initials.

EDITING

▶ **Exercise 5:** Write the capitalization and punctuation rule numbers for each correction in **bold**. Use References 11, 13, and 14 on pages 13–14 and 17–19 to look up the capitalization and punctuation rule numbers.

Did Mr. Holland, our new neighbor, drive to Dallas every Saturday in August?

▶ **Exercise 6:** Put punctuation corrections within the sentence. Write all other corrections above the sentence.
Editing Guide: Capitals: 7   Commas: 3   Apostrophes: 1   End Marks: 1

brandon annas brother stayed with his aunt mary during his visit to san diego california

Notes: _____

_____

_____

_____

_____

_____

_____

_____

_____

_____

_____

_____

_____

_____

_____

_____

_____

_____

_____

_____

_____

_____

_____

_____

_____

_____

_____

_____

_____

_____

_____

Classroom Practice 4

Name:_____ Date:_____

SKILLS

▶ **Exercise 1:** Match the definitions by writing the correct letter beside each number.

_____ 1. periods, commas, apostrophes, end marks

_____ 2. words with similar meanings

_____ 3. words with opposite meanings

_____ 4. comparisons of words with similar relationships

A. synonyms

B. antonyms

C. analogies

D. punctuation

▶ **Exercise 2:** Identify each pair of words as synonyms or antonyms by underlining the correct answer.

1. tiny, little
Synonyms or Antonyms

2. polite, rude
Synonyms or Antonyms

3. thin, thick
Synonyms or Antonyms

▶ **Exercise 3:** Choose the correct missing word and put the letter in the blank.

1. train : rain :: shell : _____	a. engine	b. beach	c. ocean	d. well
2. loud : noisy :: fast : _____	a. quick	b. bang	c. slow	d. past
3. right : wrong :: friend : _____	a. buddy	b. answer	c. enemy	d. team
4. toes : feet :: _____	a. socks : shoes	b. teeth : mouth	c. feet : heat	d. first : last

EDITING

▶ **Exercise 4:** Write the capitalization and punctuation rule numbers for each correction in **bold**. Use References 11, 13, and 14 on pages 13–14 and 17–19 to look up the capitalization and punctuation rule numbers.

Uncle Kenny's car skidded off Highway 319 during an ice storm in Texas last January.

▶ **Exercise 5:** Put punctuation corrections within the sentence. Write all other corrections above the sentence.
Editing Guide: Capitals: 8   Commas: 2   Apostrophes: 1   Misspelled Words: 1   End Marks: 1   Underline: 1

did martins teecher read the book little house on the prairie by laura ingalls wilder

Notes: _____

_____

_____

_____

_____

_____

_____

_____

_____

_____

_____

_____

_____

_____

_____

_____

_____

_____

_____

_____

_____

_____

_____

_____

_____

_____

_____

_____

_____

_____

Classroom Practice 5

Name:_____ Date:_____

GRAMMAR

▶ **Exercise 1:** Fill in the blanks below for this sentence: **Water dripped.**

1. What dripped? _____ Subject Noun _____

2. What is being said about water? _____Verb _____

3. Subject Noun, Verb, Pattern 1 _____

Classify this sentence: _____ Water dripped.

SKILLS

▶ **Exercise 2:** Identify each pair of words as synonyms or antonyms by underlining the correct answer.

1. sit, stand
Synonyms or Antonyms

2. talk, speak
Synonyms or Antonyms

3. mother, father
Synonyms or Antonyms

▶ **Exercise 3:** Choose the correct missing word and put the letter in the blank to complete the analogy.

1. up : down :: true : ___   a. under   b. blue   c. false   d. real

2. tail : monkey :: ___   a. monkey : ape   b. tail : pale   c. trunk : elephant   d. birds : tree

EDITING

▶ **Exercise 4:** Write the capitalization and punctuation rule numbers for each correction in **bold**. Use References 11, 13, and 14 on pages 13–14 and 17–19 to look up the capitalization and punctuation rule numbers.

Larry,   did   you   know   that   my   dog's   name   is   Peaches?

▶ **Exercise 5:** Put punctuation corrections within the sentence. Write all other corrections above the sentence.
Editing Guide: Capitals: 6   Commas: 2   Misspelled Words: 1   End Marks: 1

uncle ben aunt beth and grandmother came to visit us during the thanksgiving holliday

Notes: _____

_____

_____

_____

_____

_____

_____

_____

_____

_____

_____

_____

_____

_____

_____

_____

_____

_____

_____

_____

_____

_____

_____

_____

_____

_____

_____

_____

_____

Classroom Practice 6

Name:_____ Date:_____

GRAMMAR

▶ **Exercise 1:** Fill in the blanks below for this sentence: **Parents arrived very early tonight.**

1. Who arrived very early tonight? _____ Subject Noun _____

2. What is being said about parents? _____ Verb _____

3. Arrived when? _____ Adverb _____

4. How early? _____ Adverb _____

5. Arrived when? _____ Adverb _____

6. Subject Noun, Verb, Pattern 1 _____

Classify this sentence: _____ Parents arrived very early tonight.

▶ **Exercise 2:** Write the correct answers in each blank.

1. What does an adverb modify? _____

2. What does a noun name? _____

3. What are the adverb questions?_____

EDITING

▶ **Exercise 3:** Write the capitalization and punctuation rule numbers for each correction in **bold**. Use References 11, 13, and 14 on pages 13–14 and 17–19 to look up the capitalization and punctuation rule numbers.

The   Statue   of   Liberty   stands   at   the   entrance   to   New   York   Harbor.

▶ **Exercise 4:** Put punctuation corrections within the sentence. Write all other corrections above the sentence.
   Editing Guide: Capitals: 7   Commas: 2   Period: 1   End Marks: 1

mr   carter   robin   and   thomas   flew   over   the   rocky   mountains   in   colorado

SHURLEY ENGLISH

Notes: _____

_____

_____

_____

_____

_____

_____

_____

_____

_____

_____

_____

_____

_____

_____

_____

_____

_____

_____

_____

_____

_____

_____

_____

_____

_____

_____

_____

_____

_____

_____

_____

Classroom Practice 7

Name:_____ Date:_____

GRAMMAR

▶ **Exercise 1:** Fill in the blanks below for this sentence: **Several pretty butterflies flew slowly away.**

1. What flew slowly away? _____ Subject Noun _____

2. What is being said about butterflies? _____ Verb _____

3. Flew how? _____ Adverb _____

4. Flew where?_____ Adverb _____

5. What kind of butterflies? _____ Adjective _____

6. How many butterflies? _____ Adjective _____

7. Subject Noun, Verb, Pattern 1 _____

Classify this sentence: _____ Several pretty butterflies flew slowly away.

▶ **Exercise 2:** Write the correct answer in each blank.

1. What does an adverb modify? _____

2. What does an adjective modify? _____

3. What are the adverb questions? _____

4. What are the adjective questions? _____

EDITING

▶ **Exercise 3:** Write the capitalization and punctuation rule numbers for each correction in **bold**. Use References 11, 13, and 14 on pages 13–14 and 17–19 to look up the capitalization and punctuation rule numbers.

Yesterday, I read the book, <u>The Digging-est Dog</u>, by Al Perkins to my little brother.

▶ **Exercise 4:** Put punctuation corrections within the sentence. Write all other corrections above the sentence.
   Editing Guide: Capitals: 7   Commas: 1   End Marks: 1

my family and i have visited new york city the home of the statue of liberty

Notes: _____

_____

_____

_____

_____

_____

_____

_____

_____

_____

_____

_____

_____

_____

_____

_____

_____

_____

_____

_____

_____

_____

_____

_____

_____

_____

_____

_____

_____

_____

_____

Classroom Practice 8

Name:_____ Date:_____

GRAMMAR

▶ **Exercise 1:** Fill in the blanks below for this sentence. **An old teapot whistled very loudly today.**

1. What whistled very loudly today? _____Subject Noun _____

2. What is being said about teapot? _____ Verb _____

3. Whistled how? _____ Adverb _____

4. How loudly? _____ Adverb _____

5. Whistled when? _____ Adverb _____

6. What kind of teapot? _____ Adjective _____

7. _____ Article Adjective _____

8. Subject Noun, Verb, Pattern 1 _____

Classify this sentence.

_____ An old teapot whistled very loudly today.

▶ **Exercise 2:** Write the correct answers in each blank.

1. What are the article adjectives?_____

2. What does an adverb modify? _____

3. What does an adjective modify? _____

EDITING

▶ **Exercise 3:** Write the capitalization and punctuation rule numbers for each correction in **bold**. Use References 11, 13, and 14 on pages 13–14 and 17–19 to look up the capitalization and punctuation rule numbers.

My dad's favorite newspaper, <u>The New York Times</u>, is delivered to our house on Sundays.

▶ **Exercise 4:** Put punctuation corrections within the sentence. Write all other corrections above the sentence.

Editing Guide: Capitals: 6   Commas: 2   Underlining: 1   End Marks: 1

did you read the book ramona the brave by beverly cleary over the christmas holiday

Notes: _____

_____

_____

_____

_____

_____

_____

_____

_____

_____

_____

_____

_____

_____

_____

_____

_____

_____

_____

_____

_____

_____

_____

_____

_____

_____

_____

Classroom Practice 9

Name:_____ Date:_____

GRAMMAR

▶ **Exercise 1:** Fill in the blanks below for this sentence. **An extremely small candle burned very brightly.**

1. What burned very brightly?_____Subject Noun _____

2. What is being said about candle? _____ Verb _____

3. Burned how? _____Adverb _____

4. How brightly?_____Adverb _____

5. What kind of candle?_____Adjective _____

6. How small? _____Adverb _____

7. _____ Article Adjective _____

8. Subject Noun, Verb, Pattern 1 _____

9. Skill Check

10. Period, statement, declarative sentence _____

11. Go back to the verb. Divide the complete subject from the complete predicate_____

Classify this sentence.

_____   An extremely small candle burned very brightly. _____

▶ **Exercise 2:** Name the four parts of speech that you have studied so far.

1._____   2._____   3._____   4._____

SKILLS

▶ **Exercise 3:** Put the end mark and the kind of sentence in the blanks. Use these words: *declarative, exclamatory, imperative, interrogative.*

1. Josh is the winner _____   _____

2. Did you get a new CD _____   _____

3. Stay in the backyard _____   _____

4. We rode our bikes _____   _____

EDITING

▶ **Exercise 4:** Put punctuation corrections within the sentence. Write all other corrections above the sentence.
Editing Guide: Capitals: 8   Commas: 2   End Marks: 1

did chan visit his aunt in san francisco california for the chinese new year

Notes: _____

_____

_____

_____

_____

_____

_____

_____

_____

_____

_____

_____

_____

_____

_____

_____

_____

_____

_____

_____

_____

_____

_____

_____

_____

_____

_____

_____

_____

_____

Chapter 2 Checkup 10

Name:_____ Date:_____

GRAMMAR

▶ **Exercise 1:** Classify each sentence.

1. _____ Several red wasps circled angrily nearby!

2. _____ Two tiny black kittens jumped around playfully.

3. _____ A very large box arrived unexpectedly today.

▶ **Exercise 2:** Name the four parts of speech that you have studied so far.

1._____   2._____   3._____   4._____

SKILLS

▶ **Exercise 3:** Put the end mark and the kind of sentence in the blanks.
  Use these words in your answers: *declarative, exclamatory, imperative, interrogative.*

1. Do you like to fish___   _____

2. That pan is hot___   _____

3. We had tacos today___   _____

4. Clean your room___   _____

▶ **Exercise 4:** Choose the correct missing word and put the letter in the blank to complete the analogy.

1. end : begin :: hard : _____   a. finish   b. card   c. soft   d. rock

2. above : over :: leap : _____   a. under   b. frog   c. beep   d. jump

EDITING

▶ **Exercise 5:** Write the capitalization and punctuation rule numbers for each correction in **bold**. Use References
  11, 13, and 14 on pages 13–14 and 17–19 to look up the capitalization and punctuation rule numbers.

  Ray, will you come with me to Kevin's swimming party on the first Saturday in August?

▶ **Exercise 6:** Put punctuation corrections within the sentence. Write all other corrections above the sentence.
  Editing Guide: Capitals: 7   Apostrophes: 1   Periods: 1   Misspelled Words: 1   End Marks: 1

  mr   watsons   famly   is   going   camping   at   blue   rock   state   park   in   ohio

Notes: _____

Classroom Practice 11

Name: _____   Date: _____

PRACTICE & REVISED SENTENCES

1. Write a Practice Sentence according to the labels you choose.
Use the **SN V** labels once. You may use the other labels in any order and as many times as you wish in order to make a Practice Sentence.
Chapter 2 labels for a Practice Sentence: SN, V, Adj, Adv, A

2. Write a Revised Sentence. Use the following revision strategies: *synonym (syn), antonym (ant), word change (wc), added word (add), deleted word (delete), or no change (nc)*. Under each word, write the abbreviation of the revision strategy you use.

Labels:

Practice:

Revised:

Strategies:

Labels:

Practice:

Revised:

Strategies:

Labels:

Practice:

Revised:

Strategies:

Notes: _____

_____

_____

_____

_____

_____

_____

_____

_____

_____

_____

_____

_____

_____

_____

_____

_____

_____

_____

_____

_____

_____

_____

_____

_____

_____

_____

_____

_____

_____

_____

_____

_____

_____

_____

_____

Classroom Practice 12

Name:_____ Date:_____

GRAMMAR

▶ **Exercise 1:** Classify each sentence.

1. _____ Bingo slept soundly today.

2. _____ The winding mountain road curved sharply left!

3. _____ The two young squirrels chattered loudly together.

▶ **Exercise 2:** Use Sentence 1 above to complete the table below.

List the Noun Used	List the Noun Job	Singular or Plural	Common or Proper

SKILLS

▶ **Exercise 3:** Write **S** for singular or **P** for plural.

Noun	S or P
1. wolves	_____
2. otter	_____
3. wish	_____
4. cowboys	_____
5. river	_____

▶ **Exercise 4:** Write **C** for common or **P** for proper.

Noun	C or P
1. Mrs. Wong	_____
2. Friday	_____
3. Main Street	_____
4. Kansas	_____
5. street	_____

▶ **Exercise 5:** Put the end mark and the kind of sentence in the blanks.
Use these words in your answers: *declarative, exclamatory, imperative, interrogative.*

1. Did you hear the song ___   _____

2. Turn off the lights ___   _____

3. They slept in tents ___   _____

4. Dad won first prize ___   _____

EDITING

▶ **Exercise 6:** Write the capitalization and punctuation rule numbers for each correction in **bold**. Use References 11, 13, and 14 on pages 13–14 and 17–19 to look up the capitalization and punctuation rule numbers.

Tony**,** does **U**ncle **C**harles live in **F**lorida or **G**eorgia**?**

Notes: _____

_____

_____

_____

_____

_____

_____

_____

_____

_____

_____

_____

_____

_____

_____

_____

_____

_____

_____

_____

_____

_____

_____

_____

_____

_____

_____

Classroom Practice 13

Name:_____ Date:_____

GRAMMAR

▶ **Exercise 1:** Classify each sentence. Underline the complete subject once and the complete predicate twice.

1. _____ A small rescue helicopter flew quickly forward.

2. _____ The small chicken eggs hatched very slowly today.

▶ **Exercise 2:** Use Sentence 2 above to complete the table below.

List the Noun Used	List the Noun Job	Singular or Plural	Common or Proper	Simple Subject	Simple Predicate

▶ **Exercise 3:** Name the four parts of speech that you have studied so far.

1._____ 2._____ 3._____ 4._____

▶ **Exercise 4:** Underline the complete subject once and the complete predicate twice.

1. A large airplane flew noisily overhead.

2. A talented singer performed tonight.

3. A few students arrived late.

4. Several ducks swam in the pond.

▶ **Exercise 5:** Underline the simple subject once and the simple predicate twice.

1. A yellow truck traveled down the road.

2. Several black ants hurried along.

3. The little rabbit dashed across the road.

4. Amber sat quietly during class.

SKILLS

▶ **Exercise 6:** Write **S** for singular or **P** for plural.

Noun	S or P
1. houses	_____
2. table	_____
3. children	_____

▶ **Exercise 7:** Write **C** for common or **P** for proper.

Noun	C or P
1. beaver	_____
2. Willow Lake	_____
3. Mr. Jackson	_____

EDITING

▶ **Exercise 8:** Put punctuation corrections within the sentence. Write all other corrections above the sentence.

Editing Guide: Capitals: 5   Commas: 1   Periods: 1   Misspelled Words: 1   End Marks: 1

yesterday brent and pam went to dr scott to have their teeth cleened

Notes: _____

_____

_____

_____

_____

_____

_____

_____

_____

_____

_____

_____

_____

_____

_____

_____

_____

_____

_____

_____

_____

_____

_____

_____

_____

_____

_____

_____

_____

Classroom Practice 14

Name:_____ Date:_____

GRAMMAR

▶ **Exercise 1:** Classify each sentence. Underline the complete subject once and the complete predicate twice.

1. _____ Eight big green grasshoppers hopped silently around.

2. _____ Jody left very early yesterday.

▶ **Exercise 2:** Use Sentence 2 above to complete the table below.

List the Noun Used	List the Noun Job	Singular or Plural	Common or Proper	Simple Subject	Simple Predicate

SKILLS

▶ **Exercise 3:** In each column, cross out the word that does not support the underlined topic at the top.

1. **Writing Tools**	2. **Planets**	3. **Sea Animals**
pen	moon	dolphins
pencil	Earth	zebra
tape	Mars	whales

▶ **Exercise 4:** Write the name of the topic that best describes each column of words.
Choose from these topics. **Plants   Food   Drinks   Toys   Dogs   Trees**

1. _____	2. _____	3. _____
bulldog	maple	lemonade
collie	oak	tea
poodle	pine	juice

▶ **Exercise 5:** Cross out the sentence that does not support the topic.

Topic: My Little Sister

My little sister likes to play with everyone in the family. My brother chases her around. Dad tickles her, and I read to her. I read to my puppy, too. Mom plays peekaboo with my sister just before bedtime. We all kiss her goodnight. Then, she goes to sleep.

EDITING

▶ **Exercise 6:** Write the capitalization and punctuation rule numbers for each correction in **bold**. Use References 11, 13, and 14 on pages 13–14 and 17–19 to look up the capitalization and punctuation rule numbers.

Did you know that Mark Twain wrote the book, Adventures of Huckleberry Finn?

SHURLEY ENGLISH

Notes: _____

_____

_____

_____

_____

_____

_____

_____

_____

_____

_____

_____

_____

_____

_____

_____

_____

_____

_____

_____

_____

_____

_____

_____

_____

_____

_____

_____

_____

_____

Chapter 3 Checkup 15

Name:_____   Date:_____

GRAMMAR

▶ **Exercise 1:** Classify each sentence. Underline the complete subject once and the complete predicate twice.

1. _____   An   excited   newspaper   reporter   talked   very   rapidly.

2. _____   The   crowded   city   bus   stopped   too   quickly!

3. _____   An   extremely   dry   twig   snapped   sharply   nearby.

▶ **Exercise 2:** Use Sentence 1 above to complete the table below.

List the Noun Used	List the Noun Job	Singular or Plural	Common or Proper	Simple Subject	Simple Predicate

▶ **Exercise 3:** Name the four parts of speech that you have studied so far.

1._____   2._____   3._____   4._____

SKILLS

▶ **Exercise 4:** In each column, cross out the word that does not support the underlined topic at the top.

1.	**Car Parts**	2.	**Tools**	3.	**Insects**
	motor		hammer		grasshopper
	boat		wrench		bear
	wheels		paint		ladybug

▶ **Exercise 5:** Cross out the sentence that does not support the topic.

Topic: Summer Fun

During the summer, people enjoy being outside. Swimming is a favorite summer sport. For people who do not like the water, kite-flying on windy days is always fun. Baseball is enjoyed by both players and their fans. Most professional baseball players are paid a lot of money. Even watching stars is fun in the summer.

EDITING

▶ **Exercise 6:** Put punctuation corrections within the sentence. Write all other corrections above the sentence.

Editing Guide: Capitals: 5   Commas: 2   Periods: 1   End Marks: 1

ms   logan   traveled   to   springfield   missouri   on   wednesday

SHURLEY ENGLISH

Notes: _____

_____

_____

_____

_____

_____

_____

_____

_____

_____

_____

_____

_____

_____

_____

_____

_____

_____

_____

_____

_____

_____

_____

_____

_____

_____

_____

_____

Classroom Practice 16

Name: _____   Date: _____

INDEPENDENT PRACTICE & REVISED SENTENCES

1. Write a Practice Sentence according to the labels you choose.
Use the **SN V** labels once. You may use the other labels in any order and as many times as you wish in order to make a Practice Sentence.
Chapter 3 labels for a Practice Sentence: SN, **V**, Adj, Adv, A

2. Write a Revised Sentence. Use the following revision strategies: *synonym (syn)*, *antonym (ant)*, *word change (wc)*, *added word (add)*, *deleted word (delete)*, or *no change (nc)*. Under each word, write the abbreviation of the revision strategy you use.

Labels: _____

Practice: _____

Revised: _____

Strategies: _____

Labels: _____

Practice: _____

Revised: _____

Strategies: _____

Labels: _____

Practice: _____

Revised: _____

Strategies: _____

Notes: _____

_____

_____

_____

_____

_____

_____

_____

_____

_____

_____

_____

_____

_____

_____

_____

_____

_____

_____

_____

_____

_____

_____

_____

_____

_____

_____

_____

Prewriting Map

Name:_____ Date:_____

Purpose: _____

Type of Writing: _____

Audience: _____

Topic: _____

TOPIC

1ST MAIN POINT

2ND MAIN POINT

3RD MAIN POINT

SUPPORTING DETAIL

SUPPORTING DETAIL

SUPPORTING DETAIL

SUPPORTING DETAIL

SUPPORTING DETAIL

SUPPORTING DETAIL

SUPPORTING DETAIL

SUPPORTING DETAIL

SUPPORTING DETAIL

Notes: _____

_____

_____

_____

_____

_____

_____

_____

_____

_____

_____

_____

_____

_____

_____

_____

_____

_____

_____

_____

_____

_____

_____

_____

_____

_____

_____

_____

_____

Sentence Outline for an Expository Paragraph

Name:_____ Date:_____

Purpose: _____

Type of Writing: _____

Audience: _____

Topic: _____

List 3 points about the topic:

1._____ 2._____ 3._____

Sentence 1 — Write a topic and number sentence.

_____

_____

Sentence 2 — Write a three-point sentence.

_____

_____

Sentence 3 — State your first point in a complete sentence.

_____

Sentence 4 — Write a supporting sentence for the first point.

_____

_____

Sentence 5 — State your second point in a complete sentence.

_____

Sentence 6 — Write a supporting sentence for the second point.

_____

_____

Sentence 7 — State your third point in a complete sentence.

_____

Sentence 8 — Write a supporting sentence for the third point.

_____

_____

Sentence 9 — Write a concluding general sentence.

_____

_____

Notes: _____

_____

_____

_____

_____

_____

_____

_____

_____

_____

_____

_____

_____

_____

_____

_____

_____

_____

_____

_____

_____

_____

_____

_____

_____

_____

_____

_____

_____

Chapter 3 Writing Evaluation Guide

Name:_____ Date:_____

ROUGH DRAFT CHECK

_____ 1. Did you write your rough draft in pencil?

_____ 2. Did you write the correct headings on the first seven lines of your paper?

_____ 3. Did you use extra wide margins and skip every other line?

_____ 4. Did you write a title at the end of your rough draft?

_____ 5. Did you place your edited rough draft in your Rough Draft folder?

REVISING CHECK

_____ 6. Did you identify the purpose, type of writing, and audience?

_____ 7. Did you check for a topic, topic sentence, and sentences supporting the topic?

_____ 8. Did you check sentences for the right order, and did you combine, rearrange, or delete sentences when necessary?

_____ 9. Did you check for a variety of simple and compound sentences?

_____ 10. Did you check for any left out, repeated, or unnecessary words?

_____ 11. Did you check for the best choice of words by replacing or deleting unclear words?

_____ 12. Did you check the content for interest and creativity?

_____ 13. Did you check the voice to make sure the writing says what you want it to say?

EDITING CHECK

_____ 14. Did you indent each paragraph?

_____ 15. Did you circle each error and write corrections above it?

_____ 16. Did you capitalize the first word and put an end mark at the end of every sentence?

_____ 17. Did you check for all other capitalization mistakes?

_____ 18. Did you check for all punctuation mistakes?
(commas, periods, apostrophes, quotation marks, underlining)

_____ 19. Did you check for misspelled words and for incorrect homonym choices?

_____ 20. Did you check for incorrect spellings of plural and possessive forms?

_____ 21. Did you check for correct construction and punctuation of your sentences?

_____ 22. Did you check for usage mistakes? *(subject/verb agreement, a/an choices, contractions, verb tenses, degrees of adjectives, double negatives)*

_____ 23. Did you put your revised and edited paper in the Rough Draft folder?

FINAL PAPER CHECK

_____ 24. Did you write the final paper in pencil?

_____ 25. Did you center the title on the top line and center your name under the title?

_____ 26. Did you skip a line before starting the writing assignment?

_____ 27. Did you single-space, use wide margins, and write the final paper neatly?

_____ 28. Did you staple your papers in this order: final paper on top, rough draft in the middle, and prewriting map on the bottom? Did you put them in the Final Paper folder?

Notes: _____

_____

_____

_____

_____

_____

_____

_____

_____

_____

_____

_____

_____

_____

_____

_____

_____

_____

_____

_____

_____

_____

_____

_____

_____

_____

_____

_____

_____

_____

_____

Classroom Practice 17

Name:_____ Date:_____

GRAMMAR

▶ **Exercise 1:** Underline the complete subject once and the complete predicate twice.

1. _____ The old collie lay in the shade during the heat of summer.

2. _____ Several workers rode around the large zoo in small carts.

3. _____ The bear cubs in the damp cave whimpered fearfully during the storm.

▶ **Exercise 2:** Name the five parts of speech that you have studied so far.

1. _____ 2. _____ 3. _____ 4. _____ 5. _____

SKILLS

▶ **Exercise 3:** For each sentence, do three things: (1) Write the subject. (2) Write **S** and **Rule 1** if the subject is singular, or write **P** and **Rule 2** if the subject is plural. (3) Underline the correct verb.

> **Rule 1:** A singular subject must use a singular verb form that ends in **s**:
> *is, was, has, does, or other verbs ending in **s** or **es**.*
>
> **Rule 2:** A plural subject, a compound subject, or the subject **YOU** must use a plural verb form that has **no s** ending: *are, were, do, have, or verbs without **s** or **es** endings.* (A plural verb form is also called the *plain form*.)

Subject	S or P	Rule
_____	_____	_____	1. Our houses (is, are) close together.
_____	_____	_____	2. You (talks, talk) softly in the library.
_____	_____	_____	3. Dad (checks, check) the tires on the car.
_____	_____	_____	4. The kids (was, were) hiding under the bed.
_____	_____	_____	5. Jennifer and I (sleeps, sleep) upstairs.
_____	_____	_____	6. We (was, were) going to the beach.
_____	_____	_____	7. (Does, Do) Randy and Kim help with the chores?

EDITING

▶ **Exercise 4:** Write the capitalization and punctuation rule numbers for each correction in **bold**. Use References 11, 13, and 14 on pages 13–14 and 17–19 to look up the capitalization and punctuation rule numbers.

Will Mrs. Harper, our science teacher, teach about Venus, Mars, and Jupiter?

Notes: _____

_____

_____

_____

_____

_____

_____

_____

_____

_____

_____

_____

_____

_____

_____

_____

_____

_____

_____

_____

_____

_____

_____

_____

_____

_____

_____

_____

Classroom Practice 18

Name:_____ Date:_____

GRAMMAR

▶ **Exercise 1:** Classify each sentence. Underline the complete subject once and the complete predicate twice.

1. _____ The icy water flowed quickly down the mountain into the river.

2. _____ The young turtles drifted slowly in the muddy pool of water.

3. _____ Perry fell off the swing during recess!

▶ **Exercise 2:** Use Sentence 3 above to complete the table below.

List the Noun Used	List the Noun Job	Singular or Plural	Common or Proper	Simple Subject	Simple Predicate

SKILLS

▶ **Exercise 3:** For each sentence, do three things: (1) Write the subject. (2) Write **S** and **Rule 1** if the subject is singular, or write **P** and **Rule 2** if the subject is plural. (3) Underline the correct verb.

Rule 1: A singular subject must use a singular verb form that ends in **s**:
*is, was, has, does, or other verbs ending in **s** or **es**.*

Rule 2: A plural subject, a compound subject, or the subject **YOU** must use a plural verb form that has **no s** ending: *are, were, do, have, or verbs without **s** or **es** endings.* (A plural verb form is also called the *plain form.*)

Subject	S or P	Rule	
_____	_____	_____	1. The coins (shines, shine) brightly.
_____	_____	_____	2. Mary and Ron (is, are) going to the school play.
_____	_____	_____	3. You (works, work) on your homework.
_____	_____	_____	4. My friend (wasn't, weren't) going to the rodeo.
_____	_____	_____	5. (Was, Were) the tickets on sale yesterday?
_____	_____	_____	6. My brother (does, do) several card tricks.

EDITING

▶ **Exercise 4:** Put punctuation corrections within the sentence. Write all other corrections above the sentence.
Editing Guide: Capitals: 4   Commas: 3   A/An: 2   Periods: 1   End Marks: 1

today   mrs   swanson   gave   anna   her   secretary   an   bonus   for   a   outstanding   job

Notes:_____

_____

_____

_____

_____

_____

_____

_____

_____

_____

_____

_____

_____

_____

_____

_____

_____

_____

_____

_____

_____

_____

_____

_____

_____

_____

_____

_____

_____

_____

_____

Classroom Practice 19

Name:_____ Date:_____

GRAMMAR

▶ **Exercise 1:** Classify each sentence. Underline the complete subject once and the complete predicate twice.

1. _____ The beautiful woman in a long blue dress walked toward the stage.

2. _____ An old alligator lay on the muddy riverbank in the warm sun.

3. _____ The soft snowflakes drifted down to the frozen ground.

▶ **Exercise 2:** Use Sentence 3 above to complete the table below.

List the Noun Used	List the Noun Job	Singular or Plural	Common or Proper	Simple Subject	Simple Predicate

SKILLS

▶ **Exercise 3:** Write *a* or *an* in the blanks

1. He is _____ good friend.

2. ____ ripe apple fell to the ground.

3. ____ engineer

4. _____ otter is ____ animal.

5. ____ apple fell to the ground.

6. ____ train

▶ **Exercise 4:** For each sentence, do three things: (1) Write the subject. (2) Write **S** and **Rule 1** if the subject is singular, or write **P** and **Rule 2** if the subject is plural. (3) Underline the correct verb.

Subject	S or P	Rule
_____	_____	_____

1. The frisky cats (plays, play) in the barn.

2. He (doesn't, don't) want a piece of cake.

3. You (sits, sit) quietly at the dinner table.

4. Tony and Carlos always (wears, wear) a hat.

5. The woman (was, were) shopping for gifts.

6. The men in charge (hasn't, haven't) made a decision.

7. My clothes and shoes (was, were) wet from the rain.

EDITING

▶ **Exercise 5:** Write the capitalization and punctuation rule numbers for each correction in **bold**. Use References 11, 13, and 14 on pages 13–14 and 17–19 to look up the capitalization and punctuation rule numbers.

My grandfather, Mr. Daniel Miller, was born on February 22, 1952.

SHURLEY ENGLISH

Notes: _____

_____

_____

_____

_____

_____

_____

_____

_____

_____

_____

_____

_____

_____

_____

_____

_____

_____

_____

_____

_____

_____

_____

_____

_____

_____

_____

_____

Chapter 4 Checkup 20

Name:_____ Date:_____

GRAMMAR

▶ **Exercise 1:** Classify each sentence. Underline the complete subject once and the complete predicate twice.

1. _____ The long poisonous snake slithered silently through the tall, thick grass.

2. _____ Twelve green bananas ripened quickly on the shelf in the store.

3. _____ The carpenter climbed carefully down the tall ladder.

▶ **Exercise 2:** Use Sentence 2 above to complete the table below.

List the Noun Used	List the Noun Job	Singular or Plural	Common or Proper	Simple Subject	Simple Predicate

SKILLS

▶ **Exercise 3:** Write *a* or *an* in the blanks

1. Do you want _____ olive?   2. The dog chewed ____ bone.   3. ____ cup

4. _____ flute is ____ instrument.   5. The dog chewed ____ old bone.   6. ____ airplane

▶ **Exercise 4:** For each sentence, do three things: (1) Write the subject. (2) Write **S** and **Rule 1** if the subject is singular, or write **P** and **Rule 2** if the subject is plural. (3) Underline the correct verb.

Subject	S or P	Rule	
_____	_____	_____	1. You (shows, show) your dad how to use the computer.
_____	_____	_____	2. David (doesn't, don't) like spaghetti.
_____	_____	_____	3. Kelly and Casey (is, are) going to the zoo.
_____	_____	_____	4. Our canoe (glides, glide) through the water.
_____	_____	_____	5. They (was, were) caught in the storm.
_____	_____	_____	6. My friends and I (rides, ride) horses every weekend.

EDITING

▶ **Exercise 5:** Put punctuation corrections within the sentence. Write all other corrections above the sentence.
   Editing Guide: Capitals: 6   Periods: 2   End Marks: 1

was ms larson late for the meeting with mr brooks on monday

Notes: _____

_____

_____

_____

_____

_____

_____

_____

_____

_____

_____

_____

_____

_____

_____

_____

_____

_____

_____

_____

_____

_____

_____

_____

_____

_____

_____

_____

_____

Classroom Practice 21

Name: _____ Date: _____

INDEPENDENT PRACTICE & REVISED SENTENCES

1. Write a Practice Sentence according to the labels you choose.
Use the **SN V** labels once. You may use the other labels in any order and as many times as you wish in order to make a Practice Sentence.
Chapter 4 labels for a Practice Sentence: SN, V, Adj, Adv, A, P, OP

2. Write a Revised Sentence. Use the following revision strategies: *synonym (syn), antonym (ant), word change (wc), added word (add), deleted word (delete),* or *no change (nc).* Under each word, write the abbreviation of the revision strategy you use.

Labels:

Practice:

Revised:

Strategies:

Labels:

Practice:

Revised:

Strategies:

Labels:

Practice:

Revised:

Strategies:

Notes: _____

_____

_____

_____

_____

_____

_____

_____

_____

_____

_____

_____

_____

_____

_____

_____

_____

_____

_____

_____

_____

_____

_____

_____

_____

_____

_____

_____

_____

Chapter 4 Writing Evaluation Guide

Name:_____ Date:_____

ROUGH DRAFT CHECK

_____ 1. Did you write your rough draft in pencil?

_____ 2. Did you write the correct headings on the first seven lines of your paper?

_____ 3. Did you use extra wide margins and skip every other line?

_____ 4. Did you write a title at the end of your rough draft?

_____ 5. Did you place your edited rough draft in your Rough Draft folder?

REVISING CHECK

_____ 6. Did you identify the purpose, type of writing, and audience?

_____ 7. Did you check for a topic, topic sentence, and sentences supporting the topic?

_____ 8. Did you check sentences for the right order, and did you combine, rearrange, or delete sentences when necessary?

_____ 9. Did you check for a variety of simple and compound sentences?

_____ 10. Did you check for any left out, repeated, or unnecessary words?

_____ 11. Did you check for the best choice of words by replacing or deleting unclear words?

_____ 12. Did you check the content for interest and creativity?

_____ 13. Did you check the voice to make sure the writing says what you want it to say?

EDITING CHECK

_____ 14. Did you indent each paragraph?

_____ 15. Did you circle each error and write corrections above it?

_____ 16. Did you capitalize the first word and put an end mark at the end of every sentence?

_____ 17. Did you check for all other capitalization mistakes?

_____ 18. Did you check for all punctuation mistakes?
(_commas, periods, apostrophes, quotation marks, underlining_)

_____ 19. Did you check for misspelled words and for incorrect homonym choices?

_____ 20. Did you check for incorrect spellings of plural and possessive forms?

_____ 21. Did you check for correct construction and punctuation of your sentences?

_____ 22. Did you check for usage mistakes? (_subject/verb agreement, a/an choices, contractions, verb tenses, degrees of adjectives, double negatives_)

_____ 23. Did you put your revised and edited paper in the Rough Draft folder?

FINAL PAPER CHECK

_____ 24. Did you write the final paper in pencil?

_____ 25. Did you center the title on the top line and center your name under the title?

_____ 26. Did you skip a line before starting the writing assignment?

_____ 27. Did you single-space, use wide margins, and write the final paper neatly?

_____ 28. Did you staple your papers in this order: final paper on top, rough draft in the middle, and prewriting map on the bottom? Did you put them in the Final Paper folder?

Notes: _____

Classroom Practice 22

Name:_____ Date:_____

GRAMMAR

▶ **Exercise 1:** Classify each sentence. Underline the complete subject once and the complete predicate twice.

1. _____ Bees and butterflies swarmed around our flowers.

2. _____ Read very carefully for the answers to your questions.

3. _____ I ate and drank often during my train ride to Ohio.

▶ **Exercise 2:** Use Sentence 3 above to complete the table below.

List the Noun Used	List the Noun Job	Singular or Plural	Common or Proper	Simple Subject	Simple Predicate

SKILLS

▶ **Exercise 3:** Identify each type of sentence by writing the correct label in the blank. (**Labels: S, SCS, SCV**)

_____ 1. The cows and horses were in the pasture.

_____ 2. The children laughed and shouted during recess.

_____ 3. Mrs. Hill and her class went to the airport yesterday.

_____ 4. I enjoyed Brent's birthday party this afternoon.

_____ 5. The students chanted and sang songs during music class.

_____ 6. My family plants a large garden in the backyard every year.

_____ 7. Dustin and Marty went to the rodeo finals last week.

_____ 8. The big black car in the left lane stopped suddenly.

_____ 9. The children ran and played on the new equipment at the park.

_____ 10. I bought a large strawberry milkshake with whipped cream on top.

EDITING

▶ **Exercise 4:** Correct each mistake.
Editing Guide: Capitals: 8   Commas: 2   Periods: 1   Underlining: 1   End Marks: 1

yes   mr   davis   works   at   the   lincoln   star   herald   in   lincoln   nebraska

Notes: _____

_____

_____

_____

_____

_____

_____

_____

_____

_____

_____

_____

_____

_____

_____

_____

_____

_____

_____

_____

_____

_____

_____

_____

_____

_____

_____

_____

_____

Classroom Practice 23

Name:_____ Date:_____

GRAMMAR

▶ **Exercise 1:** Classify each sentence. Underline the complete subject once and the complete predicate twice.

1. _____ Look at the bright stars in the sky tonight.

2. _____ The children sing and dance in the school play.

3. _____ I worked on my science project yesterday.

▶ **Exercise 2:** Use Sentence 2 above to complete the table below.

List the Noun Used	List the Noun Job	Singular or Plural	Common or Proper	Simple Subject	Simple Predicate

SKILLS

▶ **Exercise 3:** Identify each type of sentence by writing the correct label in the blank. (**Labels: S, F, SCS, SCV**)

_____ 1. The camel can carry a big load.

_____ 2. The car bounced and bumped down the dirt road.

_____ 3. The boys and girls are listening to the ranger.

_____ 4. Ants and bees are interesting insects.

_____ 5. The students read and discussed their new books.

_____ 6. My kite got tangled in our neighbor's tree.

_____ 7. The beautiful red car in the driveway.

▶ **Exercise 4:** Use a slash to separate the two complete thoughts in each run-on sentence. Then, correct the run-on sentences by rewriting them as indicated by the labels in parentheses at the end of each sentence.

1. My dog barked loudly my dog ran after the car. (**SCV**)

_____

2. My sister played under the tree my brother played under the tree. (**SCS**)

_____

EDITING

▶ **Exercise 5:** Write the capitalization and punctuation rule numbers for each correction in **bold**. Use References 11, 13, and 14 on pages 13–14 and 17–19 to look up the capitalization and punctuation rule numbers.

Gina, have you read the book, Green Eggs and Ham, by Dr. Seuss?

SHURLEY ENGLISH

Notes: _____

Classroom Practice 24

Name:_____ Date:_____

GRAMMAR

▶ **Exercise 1:** Classify each sentence. Underline the complete subject once and the complete predicate twice.

1. _____ Stay with your aunt after school today.

2. _____ Our seeds sprouted and grew into vegetables.

3. _____ He and his friends went to the cafeteria for lunch.

▶ **Exercise 2:** Use Sentence 3 above to complete the table below.

List the Noun Used	List the Noun Job	Singular or Plural	Common or Proper	Simple Subject	Simple Predicate

SKILLS

▶ **Exercise 3:** Identify each type of sentence by writing the correct label in the blank. (**Labels: S, F, SCS, SCV**)

_____ 1. The paint can fell and spilled paint all over the floor.

_____ 2. Large pine trees grow on the side of the road.

_____ 3. My dad and I are going to the Buffalo River.

_____ 4. Roamed the countryside during the day.

_____ 5. We jumped and shouted excitedly at the game.

_____ 6. Lilly and Ben play the banjo, piano, and bass guitar.

_____ 7. Is running and exercising every evening.

▶ **Exercise 4:** Use a slash to separate the two complete thoughts in each run-on sentence. Then, correct the run-on sentences by rewriting them as indicated by the labels in parentheses at the end of each sentence.

1. Janet is a very good swimmer Chondra is a very good swimmer. (**SCS**)

_____

2. I slipped into my robe I grabbed my flashlight. (**SCV**)

_____

EDITING

▶ **Exercise 5:** Correct each mistake.
Editing Guide: Capitals: 6   Apostrophes: 2   Periods: 1   End Marks: 1

mrs smiths family celebrated grandparents day by taking nana and papa to a movie

SHURLEY ENGLISH

Notes: _____

_____

_____

_____

_____

_____

_____

_____

_____

_____

_____

_____

_____

_____

_____

_____

_____

_____

_____

_____

_____

_____

_____

_____

_____

_____

_____

Chapter 5 Checkup 25

Name:_____ Date:_____

GRAMMAR

▶ **Exercise 1:** Classify each sentence. Underline the complete subject once and the complete predicate twice.

1. _____ Ricardo and I played in the school band.

2. _____ A very loud airplane flew over our house at noon today.

3. _____ Wait patiently in line for a refill at the soda machine.

▶ **Exercise 2:** Use Sentence 1 above to complete the table below.

List the Noun Used	List the Noun Job	Singular or Plural	Common or Proper	Simple Subject	Simple Predicate

SKILLS

▶ **Exercise 3:** Identify each type of sentence by writing the correct label in the blank. (**Labels: S, F, SCS, SCV**)

_____ 1. Is talking on the phone to her friend.

_____ 2. After the game, the players and coaches celebrated.

_____ 3. Mom washed and folded our clothes.

_____ 4. All the Christmas lights look pretty at night.

_____ 5. My friends and I studied together for the big test.

▶ **Exercise 4:** Use a slash to separate the two complete thoughts in each run-on sentence. Then, correct the run-on sentences by rewriting them as indicated by the labels in parentheses at the end of each sentence.

1. My book was left in Greg's truck my computer was left in Greg's truck. (**SCS**)

_____

2. The captain of the team walked to the bench he talked to the coach. (**SCV**)

_____

EDITING

▶ **Exercise 5:** Correct each mistake.
Editing Guide: Capitals: 6 Commas: 2 Apostrophes: 1 Periods: 1 Underlining: 1 End Mark: 1

mr morris the schools librarian read the autobiography of benjamin franklin to his students

SHURLEY ENGLISH

Notes: _____

_____

_____

_____

_____

_____

_____

_____

_____

_____

_____

_____

_____

_____

_____

_____

_____

_____

_____

_____

_____

_____

_____

_____

_____

_____

_____

_____

_____

_____

_____

_____

_____

_____

Classroom Practice 26

Name: _____   Date: _____

INDEPENDENT PRACTICE & REVISED SENTENCES

1. Write a Practice Sentence according to the labels you choose.
   Use the **SN V** labels once. You may use the other labels in any order and as many times as you wish in order to make a Practice Sentence.
   Chapter 5 labels for a Practice Sentence: SN/SP, V, Adj, Adv, A, P, OP, PPA, C

2. Write a Revised Sentence. Use the following revision strategies: *synonym (syn), antonym (ant), word change (wc), added word (add), deleted word (delete),* or *no change (nc).* Under each word, write the abbreviation of the revision strategy you use.

Labels:

Practice:

Revised:

Strategies:

Labels:

Practice:

Revised:

Strategies:

Labels:

Practice:

Revised:

Strategies:

Notes: _____

_____

_____

_____

_____

_____

_____

_____

_____

_____

_____

_____

_____

_____

_____

_____

_____

_____

_____

_____

_____

_____

_____

_____

_____

_____

_____

_____

Chapter 5 Writing Evaluation Guide

Name:_____ Date:_____

ROUGH DRAFT CHECK

_____ 1. Did you write your rough draft in pencil?

_____ 2. Did you write the correct headings on the first seven lines of your paper?

_____ 3. Did you use extra wide margins and skip every other line?

_____ 4. Did you write a title at the end of your rough draft?

_____ 5. Did you place your edited rough draft in your Rough Draft folder?

REVISING CHECK

_____ 6. Did you identify the purpose, type of writing, and audience?

_____ 7. Did you check for a topic, topic sentence, and sentences supporting the topic?

_____ 8. Did you check sentences for the right order, and did you combine, rearrange, or delete sentences when necessary?

_____ 9. Did you check for a variety of simple and compound sentences?

_____ 10. Did you check for any left out, repeated, or unnecessary words?

_____ 11. Did you check for the best choice of words by replacing or deleting unclear words?

_____ 12. Did you check the content for interest and creativity?

_____ 13. Did you check the voice to make sure the writing says what you want it to say?

EDITING CHECK

_____ 14. Did you indent each paragraph?

_____ 15. Did you circle each error and write corrections above it?

_____ 16. Did you capitalize the first word and put an end mark at the end of every sentence?

_____ 17. Did you check for all other capitalization mistakes?

_____ 18. Did you check for all punctuation mistakes?
(*commas, periods, apostrophes, quotation marks, underlining*)

_____ 19. Did you check for misspelled words and for incorrect homonym choices?

_____ 20. Did you check for incorrect spellings of plural and possessive forms?

_____ 21. Did you check for correct construction and punctuation of your sentences?

_____ 22. Did you check for usage mistakes? (*subject/verb agreement, a/an choices, contractions, verb tenses, degrees of adjectives, double negatives*)

_____ 23. Did you put your revised and edited paper in the Rough Draft folder?

FINAL PAPER CHECK

_____ 24. Did you write the final paper in pencil?

_____ 25. Did you center the title on the top line and center your name under the title?

_____ 26. Did you skip a line before starting the writing assignment?

_____ 27. Did you single-space, use wide margins, and write the final paper neatly?

_____ 28. Did you staple your papers in this order: final paper on top, rough draft in the middle, and prewriting map on the bottom? Did you put them in the Final Paper folder?

SHURLEY ENGLISH

Notes: _____

_____

_____

_____

_____

_____

_____

_____

_____

_____

_____

_____

_____

_____

_____

_____

_____

_____

_____

_____

_____

_____

_____

_____

_____

Classroom Practice 27

Name:_____ Date:_____

GRAMMAR

▶ **Exercise 1:** Classify each sentence.

1. _____ Were the students listening to the guest speaker?

2. _____ After recess, he drank thirstily from a paper cup.

3. _____ I waved and shouted at the engineer of the train!

▶ **Exercise 2:** Use Sentence 1 above to complete the table below.

List the Noun Used	List the Noun Job	Singular or Plural	Common or Proper	Simple Subject	Simple Predicate

SKILLS

▶ **Exercise 3:** Identify each type of sentence by writing the correct label in the blank. (**Labels: S, F, SCS, SCV, CD**)

_____ 1. During the ballgame on Friday night.

_____ 2. My car had a flat, and it took an hour to change it.

_____ 3. The boys and girls in Ms. Jackson's class wrote a play.

_____ 4. My family went to the baseball game, and we bought hot dogs.

_____ 5. I took my puppy to the vet for his shots.

_____ 6. We can have two teams, or we can have four teams.

_____ 7. I cooked and baked for Thanksgiving dinner.

▶ **Exercise 4:** Use a slash to separate the two complete thoughts in each run-on sentence. Then, correct the run-on sentences by rewriting them as indicated by the labels in parentheses at the end of each sentence.

1. The old house caught on fire it filled with smoke. (**SCV**)

_____

2. I must study for my test I might fail. (**CD, or**)

_____

3. Ray ran for several miles Kevin ran for several miles, too. (**SCS**)

_____

EDITING

▶ **Exercise 5:** Correct each mistake.
Editing Guide: Capitals: 5   Commas: 1   Misspelled Words: 1   End Marks: 1

i   fished   at   lake   troy   and   my   frends   fished   at   flathead   lake

SHURLEY ENGLISH

Notes: _____

_____

_____

_____

_____

_____

_____

_____

_____

_____

_____

_____

_____

_____

_____

_____

_____

_____

_____

_____

_____

_____

_____

_____

_____

_____

_____

Classroom Practice 28

Name:_____ Date:_____

GRAMMAR

▶ **Exercise 1:** Classify each sentence.

1. _____ Did you swim in their pool during your summer vacation?

2. _____ Today, a squirrel scampered quickly down an oak tree for an acorn.

3. _____ Wait by the door for the church bus.

▶ **Exercise 2:** Name the seven parts of speech you have studied so far.

1._____   2._____   3._____   4._____

5._____   6._____   7._____

SKILLS

▶ **Exercise 3:** Identify each type of sentence by writing the correct label in the blank. (**Labels: S, F, SCS, SCV, CD**)

_____ 1. The children ran and played at recess.

_____ 2. You must listen, or you will not understand.

_____ 3. Elephants and whales are interesting animals.

_____ 4. Several brightly colored birds.

_____ 5. My aunt made us a pizza, and we ate it.

_____ 6. Are you meeting your friends at the movie?

▶ **Exercise 4:** Use a slash to separate each run-on sentence below. Then, correct the run-on sentences by rewriting them as indicated by the labels in parentheses at the end of each sentence.

1. I thought my sister was home she went to the mall. (**CD, but**)

_____

2. Terrance ordered hamburgers with cheese Antonio ordered the same. (**SCS**)

_____

3. The happy girl skipped down the path she also hopped down the path. (**SCV**)

_____

EDITING

▶ **Exercise 5:** Correct each mistake. **Editing Guide: End Marks: 3   Capitals: 5   Commas: 1   A/An: 1**

my family cannot agree where to go for an vacation i want to go to the beach in

florida and my brother wants to go skiing in colorado my parents want to stay home

Notes: _____

_____

_____

_____

_____

_____

_____

_____

_____

_____

_____

_____

_____

_____

_____

_____

_____

_____

_____

_____

_____

_____

_____

_____

_____

_____

_____

_____

_____

_____

_____

_____

Classroom Practice 29

Name:_____ Date:_____

GRAMMAR

▶ **Exercise 1:** Classify each sentence.

1. _____ Our coach was looking for his players in the crowded gym.

2. _____ My puppies have been barking loudly at the frogs in our pond.

3. _____ Are you going to the ballgame tonight?

▶ **Exercise 2:** Use Sentence 3 above to complete the table below.

List the Noun Used	List the Noun Job	Singular or Plural	Common or Proper	Simple Subject	Simple Predicate

SKILLS

▶ **Exercise 3:** Identify each type of sentence by writing the correct label in the blank. (**Labels: S, F, SCS, SCV, CD**)

_____ 1. My sister and I will watch TV tonight.

_____ 2. After the parade on Saturday.

_____ 3. Lindsay read a book, and Joe worked on the computer.

_____ 4. The trash was dumped and scattered.

_____ 5. Joseph spilled his milk, but he cleaned it up.

_____ 6. The teacher is leading her class outside.

▶ **Exercise 4:** Use a slash to separate each run-on sentence below. Then, correct the run-on sentences by rewriting them as indicated by the labels in parentheses at the end of each sentence.

1. Chris played the guitar Chris sang three songs. **(SCV)**

_____

2. Trent heard the whistle he did not line up. **(CD, but)**

_____

3. The parents are going on a picnic their kids are going with them. **(SCS)**

_____

EDITING

▶ **Exercise 5:** Correct each mistake. **Editing Guide: End Marks: 4   Capitals: 6   Commas: 3   Misspelled Words: 1**

i like to go to the movies with my friends sam and tyler we buy popcorn candy and

drinks we laugh and have a good time i enjoy spending time with my best freinds

Notes: _____

_____

_____

_____

_____

_____

_____

_____

_____

_____

_____

_____

_____

_____

_____

_____

_____

_____

_____

_____

_____

_____

_____

_____

_____

_____

_____

_____

Chapter 6 Checkup 30

Name:_____ Date:_____

GRAMMAR

▶ **Exercise 1:** Classify each sentence.

1. _____ Walk carefully through the crowded streets in town.

2. _____ Did you sit with Scott and Kay at the movie?

3. _____ Today, Dana and I are reading to young children at the library.

▶ **Exercise 2:** Use Sentence 2 above to complete the table below.

List the Noun Used	List the Noun Job	Singular or Plural	Common or Proper	Simple Subject	Simple Predicate

SKILLS

▶ **Exercise 3:** Identify each type of sentence by writing the correct label in the blank. (**Labels: S, F, SCS, SCV, CD**)

_____ 1. Mom's new car.

_____ 2. This game is longer than usual.

_____ 3. Mom and her sister were talking about old times.

_____ 4. I read a book, and my sister watched TV.

_____ 5. The wind whistled and howled through the trees.

▶ **Exercise 4:** Use a slash to separate each run-on sentence below. Then, correct the run-on sentences by rewriting them as indicated by the labels in parentheses at the end of each sentence.

1. Mom cooked dinner Dad washed the dishes. (**CD, and**)

_____

2. My friend likes pepperoni pizza I like pepperoni pizza. (**SCS**)

_____

3. I tripped on the rake I fell on the tomato plants. (**SCV**)

_____

EDITING

▶ **Exercise 5:** Correct each mistake.
 · **Editing Guide: End Marks: 3   Capitals: 4   Commas: 2   Apostrophes: 1   Misspelled Words: 1**

jessies little sister is learning to ride a tricycle but she does not know how to pedal she wants

someone to push her jessie is working with her every sunday so it will not take long for her to lern

Notes: _____

_____

_____

_____

_____

_____

_____

_____

_____

_____

_____

_____

_____

_____

_____

_____

_____

_____

_____

_____

_____

_____

_____

_____

_____

_____

_____

_____

Classroom Practice 31

Name: _____ Date: _____

INDEPENDENT PRACTICE & REVISED SENTENCES

1. Write a Practice Sentence according to the labels you choose.
Use the **SN V** labels once. You may use the other labels in any order and as many times as you wish in order to make a Practice Sentence.
Chapter 6 labels for a Practice Sentence: SN/SP, V, Adj, Adv, A, P, OP, PPA, C, HV

2. Write a Revised Sentence. Use the following revision strategies: *synonym (syn), antonym (ant), word change (wc), added word (add), deleted word (delete),* or *no change (nc).* Under each word, write the abbreviation of the revision strategy you use.

Labels:

Practice:

Revised:

Strategies:

Labels:

Practice:

Revised:

Strategies:

Labels:

Practice:

Revised:

Strategies:

SHURLEY ENGLISH

Notes: _____

_____

_____

_____

_____

_____

_____

_____

_____

_____

_____

_____

_____

_____

_____

_____

_____

_____

_____

_____

_____

_____

_____

_____

_____

_____

_____

Chapter 6 Writing Evaluation Guide

Name:_____ Date:_____

ROUGH DRAFT CHECK

_____ 1. Did you write your rough draft in pencil?

_____ 2. Did you write the correct headings on the first seven lines of your paper?

_____ 3. Did you use extra wide margins and skip every other line?

_____ 4. Did you write a title at the end of your rough draft?

_____ 5. Did you place your edited rough draft in your Rough Draft folder?

REVISING CHECK

_____ 6. Did you identify the purpose, type of writing, and audience?

_____ 7. Did you check for a topic, topic sentence, and sentences supporting the topic?

_____ 8. Did you check sentences for the right order, and did you combine, rearrange, or delete sentences when necessary?

_____ 9. Did you check for a variety of simple and compound sentences?

_____ 10. Did you check for any left out, repeated, or unnecessary words?

_____ 11. Did you check for the best choice of words by replacing or deleting unclear words?

_____ 12. Did you check the content for interest and creativity?

_____ 13. Did you check the voice to make sure the writing says what you want it to say?

EDITING CHECK

_____ 14. Did you indent each paragraph?

_____ 15. Did you circle each error and write corrections above it?

_____ 16. Did you capitalize the first word and put an end mark at the end of every sentence?

_____ 17. Did you check for all other capitalization mistakes?

_____ 18. Did you check for all punctuation mistakes?
(commas, periods, apostrophes, quotation marks, underlining)

_____ 19. Did you check for misspelled words and for incorrect homonym choices?

_____ 20. Did you check for incorrect spellings of plural and possessive forms?

_____ 21. Did you check for correct construction and punctuation of your sentences?

_____ 22. Did you check for usage mistakes? *(subject/verb agreement, a/an choices, contractions, verb tenses, degrees of adjectives, double negatives)*

_____ 23. Did you put your revised and edited paper in the Rough Draft folder?

FINAL PAPER CHECK

_____ 24. Did you write the final paper in pencil?

_____ 25. Did you center the title on the top line and center your name under the title?

_____ 26. Did you skip a line before starting the writing assignment?

_____ 27. Did you single-space, use wide margins, and write the final paper neatly?

_____ 28. Did you staple your papers in this order: final paper on top, rough draft in the middle, and prewriting map on the bottom? Did you put them in the Final Paper folder?

Notes: _____

_____

_____

_____

_____

_____

_____

_____

_____

_____

_____

_____

_____

_____

_____

_____

_____

_____

_____

_____

_____

_____

_____

_____

_____

_____

_____

_____

_____

_____

Classroom Practice 32

Name:_____ Date:_____

GRAMMAR

▶ **Exercise 1:** Classify each sentence.

1. _____ They looked for Andrew's kite for several hours.

2. _____ Ouch! That bee sting hurts!

3. _____ Wave to the circus clowns.

▶ **Exercise 2:** Use Sentence 1 above to complete the table below.

List the Noun Used	List the Noun Job	Singular or Plural	Common or Proper	Simple Subject	Simple Predicate

SKILLS

▶ **Exercise 3:** Underline the correct homonym in each sentence.

1. The (new, knew) computer arrived early.

2. Will you (pore, pour) me a cup of coffee?

3. The (sea, see) is calm at dusk.

4. The skunk's (cent, scent) is very strong.

5. We (no, know) our multiplication tables.

6. The refrigerators cost (to, too, two) much.

▶ **Exercise 4:** Use a slash to separate each run-on sentence below. Then, correct the run-on sentences by rewriting them as indicated by the labels in parentheses at the end of each sentence.

1. The puppies ran around the puppies rolled in the grass. (SCV)

_____

2. He came to dinner he did not eat. (CD, but)

_____

3. The butterflies flew around the flowers the honeybees flew around the flowers. (SCS)

_____

EDITING

▶ **Exercise 5:** Correct each mistake.
   Editing Guide: **End Marks: 3   Capitals: 7   Commas: 2   Homonyms: 4   Apostrophes: 1   A/An: 1**

i love eating at grandmas house and i eat their every friday night she makes the best roles

and i always eat fore of them grandma lives in an little blue house write across the street from me

Notes: _____

_____

_____

_____

_____

_____

_____

_____

_____

_____

_____

_____

_____

_____

_____

_____

_____

_____

_____

_____

_____

_____

_____

_____

_____

_____

_____

_____

Classroom Practice 33

Name:_____ Date:_____

GRAMMAR

▶ **Exercise 1:** Classify each sentence.

1. _____ Yesterday, the children laughed gleefully at their uncle's jokes.

2. _____ Oh, no! Our neighbor's house across the street burned down!

3. _____ Did the bold young redbird fly to my feeder yesterday?

SKILLS

▶ **Exercise 2:** Write either the contraction or the contraction words in the blanks.

1. I am _____   4. has not _____   7. he's _____

2. is not _____   5. you have _____   8. they've _____

3. will not _____   6. you will _____   9. he'd _____

▶ **Exercise 3:** Underline the correct homonym in each sentence.

1. The students are in the (forth, fourth) grade.   4. He was (weak, week) after surgery.

2. Do you want a (peace, piece) of cake?   5. The children (blue, blew) lots of bubbles.

3. The wound did not (heal, heel) properly.   6. Are we meeting (hear, here) today?

▶ **Exercise 4:** Identify each type of sentence by writing the correct label in the blank. (**Labels: S, F, SCS, SCV, CD**)

_____ 1. I want to go to the lake, but I have to work.

_____ 2. Fred and Jennifer bought groceries yesterday.

_____ 3. We shopped for dishes and towels.

_____ 4. The chocolate fudge on the counter.

_____ 5. The nurse listened and asked questions.

EDITING

▶ **Exercise 5:** Correct each mistake.
Editing Guide: End Marks: 4   Capitals: 5   Commas: 2   Homonyms: 2   Apostrophes: 3   A/An: 1   Misspelled Words: 1

    i dont understand my brother he likes two bee around me and he follows me everwhere

he talks all the time and i dont understand an word why cant two-year olds leave sisters alone

Notes: _____

_____

_____

_____

_____

_____

_____

_____

_____

_____

_____

_____

_____

_____

_____

_____

_____

_____

_____

_____

_____

_____

_____

_____

_____

_____

_____

_____

_____

_____

_____

Classroom Practice 34

Name:_____ Date:_____

GRAMMAR

▶ **Exercise 1:** Classify each sentence.

1. _____ Yea! Our team has won again!

2. _____ Yesterday, the town parade passed by my father's store.

3. _____ The rooster and chickens pecked around the chicken yard.

SKILLS

▶ **Exercise 2:** Write either the contraction or the contraction words in the blanks.

1. are not _____   4. had not _____   7. we'll _____

2. you are _____   5. he has _____   8. won't _____

3. do not _____   6. was not _____   9. let's _____

▶ **Exercise 3:** Underline the correct homonym in each sentence.

1. He parked (buy, by) the (blew, blue) van.   4. He used the (right, write) forms.

2. Did you go (threw, through) the tunnel?   5. The raccoon hurt (its, it's) foot.

3. The (son, sun) is bright today.   6. The (lead, led) pipe was bent.

▶ **Exercise 4:** Identify each type of sentence by writing the correct label in the blank. (**Labels: S, F, SCS, SCV, CD**)

_____ 1. We drove all day and spent the night in Ohio.

_____ 2. The geese are flying south for the winter.

_____ 3. Damaged several houses in our community.

_____ 4. My dad and his brothers work together on the farm.

_____ 5. The baby was very sleepy, and she took a long nap.

EDITING

▶ **Exercise 5:** Correct each mistake.
  Editing Guide: **End Marks: 4   Capitals: 6   Homonyms: 6   Apostrophes: 2   A/An: 1   Period: 1**

we do not want to sea an skunk under our knew house its scent is two strong for us we dont

want to meet mr skunks wife or there family we want piece and quiet around hear

SHURLEY ENGLISH

Notes: _____

_____

_____

_____

_____

_____

_____

_____

_____

_____

_____

_____

_____

_____

_____

_____

_____

_____

_____

_____

_____

_____

_____

_____

_____

_____

_____

_____

_____

_____

Chapter 7 Checkup 35

Name:_____ Date:_____

GRAMMAR

▶ **Exercise 1:** Classify each sentence.

1. _____ Look at the two hungry rabbits in the vegetable garden.

2. _____ Yesterday, my mother's friends and neighbors arrived in time for the surprise party.

3. _____ Oops! My homemade kite landed in the pond by the barn!

SKILLS

▶ **Exercise 2:** Write either the contraction or the contraction words in the blanks.

1. they are _____   4. she will _____   7. there's _____

2. she had _____   5. it is _____   8. she's _____

3. cannot_____   6. I will _____   9. haven't _____

▶ **Exercise 3:** Underline the correct homonym in each sentence.

1. Our guide (lead, led) the way.   4. Jason will need (fore, four) pencils.

2. (Your, You're) going with me.   5. My (knew, new) bike is (blue, blew).

3. She is the (principle, principal) of our school.   6. I can't wait to (meat, meet) your aunt.

▶ **Exercise 4:** Identify each type of sentence by writing the correct label in the blank. (**Labels: S, F, SCS, SCV, CD**)

_____ 1. The lost children were quite frightened.

_____ 2. Zack and I ordered ham and eggs.

_____ 3. Our team lost, but they played a good game.

_____ 4. I grabbed my keys and ran to the car.

_____ 5. Carefully to the words of the song.

EDITING

▶ **Exercise 5:** Correct each mistake. **Editing Guide: End Marks: 4   Capitals: 7   Homonyms: 5   Apostrophes: 1   A/An: 1**

we drove threw a tunnel and stopped at a interesting store two eat big mike and big

mona owned the place they gave us a peace of pie and told us there story we had fun and

didnt want too leave

SHURLEY ENGLISH

Notes: _____

_____

_____

_____

_____

_____

_____

_____

_____

_____

_____

_____

_____

_____

_____

_____

_____

_____

_____

_____

_____

_____

_____

_____

_____

_____

_____

_____

_____

Classroom Practice 36

Name: _____   Date: _____

INDEPENDENT PRACTICE & REVISED SENTENCES

1. Write a Practice Sentence according to the labels you choose.
Use the SN\SP V labels once. You may use the other labels in any order and as many times as you wish in order to make a Practice Sentence.
Chapter 7 labels for a Practice Sentence: SN\SP, V, Adj, Adv, A, P, OP, PPA, C, HV, I, and PNA

2. Write a Revised Sentence. Use the following revision strategies: *synonym (syn), antonym (ant), word change (wc), added word (add), deleted word (delete),* or *no change (nc).* Under each word, write the abbreviation of the revision strategy you use.

Labels:

Practice:

Revised:

Strategies:

Labels:

Practice:

Revised:

Strategies:

Labels:

Practice:

Revised:

Strategies:

Notes: _____

_____

_____

_____

_____

_____

_____

_____

_____

_____

_____

_____

_____

_____

_____

_____

_____

_____

_____

_____

_____

_____

_____

_____

_____

_____

Chapter 7 Writing Evaluation Guide

Name:_____ Date:_____

ROUGH DRAFT CHECK

_____ 1. Did you write your rough draft in pencil?

_____ 2. Did you write the correct headings on the first seven lines of your paper?

_____ 3. Did you use extra wide margins and skip every other line?

_____ 4. Did you write a title at the end of your rough draft?

_____ 5. Did you place your edited rough draft in your Rough Draft folder?

REVISING CHECK

_____ 6. Did you identify the purpose, type of writing, and audience?

_____ 7. Did you check for a topic, topic sentence, and sentences supporting the topic?

_____ 8. Did you check sentences for the right order, and did you combine, rearrange, or delete sentences when necessary?

_____ 9. Did you check for a variety of simple and compound sentences?

_____ 10. Did you check for any left out, repeated, or unnecessary words?

_____ 11. Did you check for the best choice of words by replacing or deleting unclear words?

_____ 12. Did you check the content for interest and creativity?

_____ 13. Did you check the voice to make sure the writing says what you want it to say?

EDITING CHECK

_____ 14. Did you indent each paragraph?

_____ 15. Did you circle each error and write corrections above it?

_____ 16. Did you capitalize the first word and put an end mark at the end of every sentence?

_____ 17. Did you check for all other capitalization mistakes?

_____ 18. Did you check for all punctuation mistakes?
(commas, periods, apostrophes, quotation marks, underlining)

_____ 19. Did you check for misspelled words and for incorrect homonym choices?

_____ 20. Did you check for incorrect spellings of plural and possessive forms?

_____ 21. Did you check for correct construction and punctuation of your sentences?

_____ 22. Did you check for usage mistakes? (subject/verb agreement, a/an choices, contractions, verb tenses, degrees of adjectives, double negatives)

_____ 23. Did you put your revised and edited paper in the Rough Draft folder?

FINAL PAPER CHECK

_____ 24. Did you write the final paper in pencil?

_____ 25. Did you center the title on the top line and center your name under the title?

_____ 26. Did you skip a line before starting the writing assignment?

_____ 27. Did you single-space, use wide margins, and write the final paper neatly?

_____ 28. Did you staple your papers in this order: final paper on top, rough draft in the middle, and prewriting map on the bottom? Did you put them in the Final Paper folder?

Notes: _____

_____

_____

_____

_____

_____

_____

_____

_____

_____

_____

_____

_____

_____

_____

_____

_____

_____

_____

_____

_____

_____

_____

_____

_____

_____

_____

_____

_____

_____

_____

_____

Classroom Practice 37

Name:_____ Date:_____

GRAMMAR

▶ **Exercise 1:** Classify each sentence.

1. _____ Travis built a small boat.

2. _____ The workers painted our house.

3. _____ Jill baked a cake for the party.

▶ **Exercise 2:** Use Sentence 3 to complete the table below.

List the Noun Used	List the Noun Job	Singular or Plural	Common or Proper	Simple Subject	Simple Predicate

SKILLS

▶ **Exercise 3:** (1) Underline the verb or verb phrase. (2) Identify the verb tense by writing **1** for present tense, **2** for past tense, or **3** for future tense. (3) Write the past-tense form. (4) Write **R** for Regular or **I** for Irregular.

	Verb Tense	Main Verb Past Tense Form	R or I
1. Brent cleans the car every Saturday.			
2. My cousin gave candy to us after dinner.			
3. Every person will go on the train ride.			
4. The front door closed with a bang.			
5. Will flowers grow in the garden?			
6. Those cookies smell delicious.			
7. The children sing in the choir.			
8. Our collie will play fetch with you.			

EDITING

▶ **Exercise 4:** Correct each mistake.
  Editing Guide: **End Marks: 4** **Capitals: 8** **Commas: 3** **Apostrophes: 2** **A/An: 1** **Misspelled Words: 1**

abby loves her little dog mopsey she plays with him every day abbys father tickles

mopsey on his tummy and her mother gives him an treat at night mopsey jumps in abbys lap

and snuggles happily

Notes: _____

_____

_____

_____

_____

_____

_____

_____

_____

_____

_____

_____

_____

_____

_____

_____

_____

_____

_____

_____

_____

_____

_____

_____

_____

_____

Classroom Practice 38

Name:_____ Date:_____

GRAMMAR

▶ **Exercise 1:** Classify each sentence.

1. _____ Today, Dad ate two eggs and bacon for breakfast.

2. _____ Does Nathan empty the trash after school?

3. _____ Bring your new friend to our family picnic.

▶ **Exercise 2:** Use Sentence 1 above to complete the table below.

List the Noun Used	List the Noun Job	Singular or Plural	Common or Proper	Simple Subject	Simple Predicate

SKILLS

▶ **Exercise 3:** (1) Underline the verb or verb phrase. (2) Identify the verb tense by writing **1** for present tense, **2** for past tense, or **3** for future tense. (3) Write the past-tense form. (4) Write **R** for Regular or **I** for Irregular.

	Verb Tense	Main Verb Past Tense Form	R or I
1. Sandra is waiting for her mother.			
2. Those children will choose red paint.			
3. The fans rushed onto the field after the game.			
4. My mom gives away her homemade jelly.			
5. Sam did not write his name on his paper.			
6. Amanda and I have talked on the phone.			

▶ **Exercise 4:** List the present-tense and past-tense helping verbs below. (These verbs are listed in Reference 120.)

Present Tense	1.	2.	3.	4.	5.	6.	7.
Past Tense	1.	2.	3.	4.	5.		

EDITING

▶ **Exercise 5:** Correct each mistake. **Editing Guide: End Marks: 5   Capitals: 5   Commas: 2   Homonyms: 3**

jeffery looked at the sky it was getting darker and he could here the thunder he new it

would rain soon he went threw the house and closed all the windows then the rain poured down

SHURLEY ENGLISH

Notes: _____

_____

_____

_____

_____

_____

_____

_____

_____

_____

_____

_____

_____

_____

_____

_____

_____

_____

_____

_____

_____

_____

_____

_____

_____

_____

_____

_____

_____

_____

Classroom Practice 39

Name:_____ Date:_____

GRAMMAR

▶ **Exercise 1:** Classify each sentence.

1. _____ Shelly cleaned the carpet in her bedroom today.

2. _____ Hurray! The Panthers won their final soccer game!

3. _____ At her graduation, Molly gave an outstanding speech.

SKILLS

▶ **Exercise 2:** (1) Underline the verb or verb phrase. (2) Identify the verb tense by writing **1** for present tense, **2** for past tense, or **3** for future tense. (3) Write the past-tense form. (4) Write **R** for Regular or **I** for Irregular.

	Verb Tense	Main Verb Past Tense Form	R or I
1. Kendrell is moving the books to a lower shelf.			
2. A grasshopper was eating our tomato plant.			
3. Will Dad talk to us before dinner?			
4. The hens sit on their nests.			
5. He has walked two miles.			
6. Cindy will go to the library.			
7. My friends were singing in the car.			
8. Dana is waiting for her mother.			
9. He rode the train to the city.			

▶ **Exercise 3:** List the present-tense and past-tense helping verbs below.

Present Tense	1.	2.	3.	4.	5.	6.	7.
Past Tense	1.	2.	3.	4.	5.		

EDITING

▶ **Exercise 4:** Correct each mistake. Editing Guide: **End Marks: 4   Capitals: 6   Commas: 5   Homonyms: 2   A/An: 1**

jalene ordered garden seeds from an store in dallas texas to plant in her knew garden she

dug neat little rows dropped the seeds in and covered them up she watched the seeds grow into

vegetables she invited her friends over to sea her garden and she gave them fresh tomatoes

SHURLEY ENGLISH

Notes: _____

_____

_____

_____

_____

_____

_____

_____

_____

_____

_____

_____

_____

_____

_____

_____

_____

_____

_____

_____

_____

_____

_____

_____

_____

_____

_____

_____

_____

Chapter 8 Checkup 40

Name:_____ Date:_____

GRAMMAR

▶ **Exercise 1:** Classify each sentence.

1. _____ Put some cheese slices and bread on your plate.

2. _____ Before dinner, Terry and I played a quick game of cards.

3. _____ Did Clint's son change the damaged tire on their car?

SKILLS

▶ **Exercise 2:** (1) Underline the verb or verb phrase. (2) Identify the verb tense by writing **1** for present tense, **2** for past tense, or **3** for future tense. (3) Write the past-tense form. (4) Write **R** for Regular or **I** for Irregular.

	Verb Tense	Main Verb Past Tense Form	R or I
1. Colorful leaves fall in my yard in October.			
2. Kerry closed the door very quietly.			
3. My friends are listening to music.			
4. Will you tell my mother your recipe?			
5. Tyson is blowing the whistle loudly.			
6. Grandma has bought groceries this week.			
7. The puppy whined for a playmate.			
8. Everyone was laughing at his jokes.			
9. My dad and mom will see a movie tonight.			

▶ **Exercise 3:** List the present-tense and past-tense helping verbs below.

Present Tense	1.	2.	3.	4.	5.	6.	7.
Past Tense	1.	2.	3.	4.	5.		

EDITING

▶ **Exercise 4:** Correct each mistake.
Editing Guide: End Marks: 3   Capitals: 5   Commas: 1   Homonyms: 2   Apostrophes: 2

dales little kitten would play with his mothers ball of yarn for ours dale and his mother

watched trixie and laughed at the funny things she did then trixie would walk away with her

tail inn the air and lay daintily on her pillow

Notes: _____

_____

_____

_____

_____

_____

_____

_____

_____

_____

_____

_____

_____

_____

_____

_____

_____

_____

_____

_____

_____

_____

_____

_____

_____

_____

_____

_____

_____

Classroom Practice 41

Name: _____

Date: _____

INDEPENDENT PRACTICE & REVISED SENTENCES

1. Write a Practice Sentence according to the labels you choose.

Use **SN/SP V-t DO** as your main labels. You may use the other labels in any order and as many times as you wish in order to make a Practice Sentence. **Chapter 8 labels for a Practice Sentence: SN/SP, V-t, DO,** Adj, Adv, A, P, OP, PPA, C, HV, I, PNA

2. Write a Revised Sentence. Use the following revision strategies: *synonym (syn), antonym (ant), word change (wc), added word (add), deleted word (delete),* or *no change (nc).* Under each word, write the abbreviation of the revision strategy you use.

Labels: _____

Practice: _____

Revised: _____

Strategies: _____

Labels: _____

Practice: _____

Revised: _____

Strategies: _____

Labels: _____

Practice: _____

Revised: _____

Strategies: _____

SHURLEY ENGLISH

Notes: _____

_____

_____

_____

_____

_____

_____

_____

_____

_____

_____

_____

_____

_____

_____

_____

_____

_____

_____

_____

_____

_____

_____

_____

_____

_____

_____

_____

Chapter 8 Writing Evaluation Guide

Name:_____ Date:_____

ROUGH DRAFT CHECK

_____ 1. Did you write your rough draft in pencil?

_____ 2. Did you write the correct headings on the first seven lines of your paper?

_____ 3. Did you use extra wide margins and skip every other line?

_____ 4. Did you write a title at the end of your rough draft?

_____ 5. Did you place your edited rough draft in your Rough Draft folder?

REVISING CHECK

_____ 6. Did you identify the purpose, type of writing, and audience?

_____ 7. Did you check for a topic, topic sentence, and sentences supporting the topic?

_____ 8. Did you check sentences for the right order, and did you combine, rearrange, or delete sentences when necessary?

_____ 9. Did you check for a variety of simple and compound sentences?

_____ 10. Did you check for any left out, repeated, or unnecessary words?

_____ 11. Did you check for the best choice of words by replacing or deleting unclear words?

_____ 12. Did you check the content for interest and creativity?

_____ 13. Did you check the voice to make sure the writing says what you want it to say?

EDITING CHECK

_____ 14. Did you indent each paragraph?

_____ 15. Did you circle each error and write corrections above it?

_____ 16. Did you capitalize the first word and put an end mark at the end of every sentence?

_____ 17. Did you check for all other capitalization mistakes?

_____ 18. Did you check for all punctuation mistakes?
(commas, periods, apostrophes, quotation marks, underlining)

_____ 19. Did you check for misspelled words and for incorrect homonym choices?

_____ 20. Did you check for incorrect spellings of plural and possessive forms?

_____ 21. Did you check for correct construction and punctuation of your sentences?

_____ 22. Did you check for usage mistakes? _(subject/verb agreement, a/an choices, contractions, verb tenses, degrees of adjectives, double negatives)_

_____ 23. Did you put your revised and edited paper in the Rough Draft folder?

FINAL PAPER CHECK

_____ 24. Did you write the final paper in pencil?

_____ 25. Did you center the title on the top line and center your name under the title?

_____ 26. Did you skip a line before starting the writing assignment?

_____ 27. Did you single-space, use wide margins, and write the final paper neatly?

_____ 28. Did you staple your papers in this order: final paper on top, rough draft in the middle, and prewriting map on the bottom? Did you put them in the Final Paper folder?

Notes: _____

_____

_____

_____

_____

_____

_____

_____

_____

_____

_____

_____

_____

_____

_____

_____

_____

_____

_____

_____

_____

_____

_____

_____

_____

_____

_____

_____

_____

Classroom Practice 42

Name:_____ Date:_____

GRAMMAR

▶ **Exercise 1:** Classify each sentence.

1. _____ Will the funny clowns at the circus ride in a tiny car?

2. _____ Tony and Brad tripped over the fishing gear and fell into the water!

3. _____ Fly your paper airplanes outside today.

▶ **Exercise 2:** Use Sentence 3 above to complete the table below.

List the Noun Used	List the Noun Job	Singular or Plural	Common or Proper	Simple Subject	Simple Predicate

SKILLS

▶ **Exercise 3:** Change the underlined present-tense verbs in Paragraph 1 to past-tense verbs in Paragraph 2.

Paragraph 1: Present Tense

Dad's old lawnmower **coughs** and **sputters** as it **struggles** to cut a path through the tall green grass. The blades **stop** each time Dad **comes** to an especially thick patch of grass. Row by row, Dad **pushes** the mower gently through the grass. The grass **is changed** into a neat, green carpet. Dad **is** at the end of his last row when the lawnmower **dies**. A huge cloud of smoke **rolls** from the mower.

Paragraph 2: Past Tense

Dad's old lawnmower _____ and _____ as it _____ to cut a path through the tall green grass. The blades _____ each time Dad _____ to an especially thick patch of grass. Row by row, Dad _____ the mower gently through the grass. The grass _____ _____ into a neat, green carpet. Dad _____ at the end of his last row when the lawnmower _____. A huge cloud of smoke _____ from the mower.

EDITING

▶ **Exercise 4:** Correct each mistake. **Editing Guide:** **End Marks: 1** **Capitals: 9** **Commas: 3**

matt chris and amber play the french horn at garland high school in portland oregon

Notes: _____

_____

_____

_____

_____

_____

_____

_____

_____

_____

_____

_____

_____

_____

_____

_____

_____

_____

_____

_____

_____

_____

_____

_____

_____

_____

_____

_____

_____

_____

_____

Classroom Practice 43

Name:_____ Date:_____

GRAMMAR

▶ **Exercise 1:** Classify each sentence.

1. _____ Lead me to the hidden cave in the mountains.

2. _____ Did the businessman at the mall buy a new suit?

3. _____ The colorful kites flew high in the sky above us.

SKILLS

▶ **Exercise 2:** Change the underlined mixed-tense verbs in Paragraph 1 to the tense listed for Paragraph 2.

Paragraph 1: Mixed Tense

    My brother **found** a snake by the garage. He **yells** excitedly for everyone. Everyone **came** very fast. We all **stood** back until Dad **looks** at the snake very carefully. The snake **is** only a little garden snake this time. But my brother **was** wise when he **called** for an older person. My dad **is** proud of him and **tells** him so. My brother **grinned** and **walks** off. He **is looking** for another snake!

Paragraph 2: Present Tense

    My brother _____ a snake by the garage. He _____ excitedly for everyone. Everyone _____ very fast. We all _____ back until Dad _____ at the snake very carefully. The snake _____ only a little garden snake this time. But my brother _____ wise when he _____ for an older person. My dad _____ proud of him and _____ him so. My brother _____ and _____ off. He _____ _____ for another snake!

EDITING

▶ **Exercise 3:** Correct each mistake.

        Editing Guide: End Marks: 1   Capitals: 7   Commas: 4   A/An: 1   Misspelled Words: 1

during the civil war harriet tubman served in the union army as an cook nurs scout and spy

Notes: _____

_____

_____

_____

_____

_____

_____

_____

_____

_____

_____

_____

_____

_____

_____

_____

_____

_____

_____

_____

_____

_____

_____

_____

_____

_____

_____

_____

_____

Classroom Practice 44

Name:_____ Date:_____

GRAMMAR

▶ **Exercise 1:** Classify each sentence.

1. _____ Kay sang and danced for her talent in the talent search.

2. _____ Take them quietly to the kitchen for a snack.

3. _____ Rosa drives a little white car to work.

SKILLS

▶ **Exercise 2:** Change the underlined mixed-tense verbs in Paragraph 1 to the tense listed for Paragraph 2.

Paragraph 1: Mixed Tense

Mom always **asks** me to get everything ready for school the night before. First, I **selected** the clothes I **want** to wear. Next, I **gather** my school things into my bookbag and **placed** it by the front door. Then, I **take** my bath and **brushed** my teeth. Finally, I **crawl** sleepily into bed. I **love** getting organized because it **made** every morning great!

Paragraph 2: Past Tense

Mom always _____ me to get everything ready for school the night before. First, I _____ the clothes I _____ to wear. Next, I _____ my school things into my bookbag and _____ it by the front door. Then, I _____ my bath and _____ my teeth. Finally, I _____ sleepily into bed. I _____ getting organized because it _____ every morning great!

EDITING

▶ **Exercise 3:** Correct each mistake. **Editing Guide: End Marks: 1   Capitals: 7   Commas: 1   A/An: 1**

orville and wilbur wright flew the first airplane at an beach in kitty hawk north carolina

SHURLEY ENGLISH

Notes: _____

_____

_____

_____

_____

_____

_____

_____

_____

_____

_____

_____

_____

_____

_____

_____

_____

_____

_____

_____

_____

_____

_____

_____

_____

_____

_____

_____

_____

_____

Classroom Practice 45

Name:_____ Date:_____

GRAMMAR

▶ **Exercise 1:** Classify each sentence.

1. _____ My aunt will make her famous fudge for us at Christmas.

2. _____ I closed my eyes during the scary part of the movie.

3. _____ An old, sleepy lion at the zoo yawned lazily at me.

SKILLS

▶ **Exercise 2:** Change the underlined mixed-tense verbs in Paragraph 1 to the tense listed for Paragraph 2.

Paragraph 1: Mixed Tense

My family **bought** me a new puppy. I **name** him Rufus. Rufus **sniffs** everything and **ran** all around his new home. We **had** a great time. But when night **comes**, Rufus **missed** his mother. He **cries** a lot. My mom **takes** an alarm clock and a hot water bottle to Rufus's room. She **placed** them under his blanket. Rufus **went** right to sleep because these things **remind** him of his mother!

Paragraph 2: Present Tense

My family _____ me a new puppy. I _____ him

Rufus. Rufus _____ everything and _____ all around

his new home. We _____ a great time. But when night _____,

Rufus _____ his mother. He _____ a lot. My mom

_____ an alarm clock and a hot water bottle to Rufus's room. She

_____ them under his blanket. Rufus _____ right to

sleep because these things _____ him of his mother!

EDITING

▶ **Exercise 3:** Correct each mistake. **Editing Guide: End Marks: 1   Capitals: 7   Commas: 4   Homonyms: 1**

justin dean and i are going too fairbanks alaska with grandmother in august

SHURLEY ENGLISH

Notes: _____

_____

_____

_____

_____

_____

_____

_____

_____

_____

_____

_____

_____

_____

_____

_____

_____

_____

_____

_____

_____

_____

_____

_____

_____

_____

_____

_____

_____

_____

_____

_____

Chapter 9 Checkup 46

Name:_____ Date:_____

GRAMMAR

▶ **Exercise 1:** Classify each sentence.

1. _____ Dad and I built and painted a dollhouse for my little sister.

2. _____ Save a piece of chocolate cake for Mandy and him.

3. _____ After school, Scott walked to my office and talked to me.

SKILLS

▶ **Exercise 2:** Change the underlined mixed-tense verbs in Paragraph 1 to the tense listed for Paragraph 2.

Paragraph 1: Mixed Tense

My friends and I **were playing** jump rope on the sidewalk in front of our apartments. We **wave** at our dads as they **drove** up from work. They **laugh** as they **watched** us, so we **handed** them the rope. They all **get** in line and **jumped**. Everyone **clapped** and **cheers** for our dads. They **grin** and **bowed**. Then, they **wiped** their foreheads and **hand** the rope back to us. We **giggle** as they **limped** into the building.

Paragraph 2: Present Tense

My friends and I _____ _____ jump rope on the sidewalk

in front of our apartments. We _____ at our dads as they

_____ up from work. They _____ as they

_____ us, so we _____ them the rope. They all

_____ in line and _____. Everyone

_____ and _____ for our dads. They

_____ and _____. Then, they

_____ their foreheads and _____ the rope back to

us. We _____ as they _____ into the building.

EDITING

▶ **Exercise 3:** Correct each mistake.

Editing Guide: End Marks: 1   Periods: 2   Capitals: 6   Commas: 2   Homonyms: 1   Apostrophes: 1   Misspelled Words: 1

mr   walker   took   polly   his   talking   parrot   too   dr   chapmans   office   on   saterday

Notes: _____

_____

_____

_____

_____

_____

_____

_____

_____

_____

_____

_____

_____

_____

_____

_____

_____

_____

_____

_____

_____

_____

_____

_____

_____

_____

_____

_____

_____

_____

Chapter 9 Writing Evaluation Guide

Name:_____ Date:_____

ROUGH DRAFT CHECK

_____ 1. Did you write your rough draft in pencil?

_____ 2. Did you write the correct headings on the first seven lines of your paper?

_____ 3. Did you use extra wide margins and skip every other line?

_____ 4. Did you write a title at the end of your rough draft?

_____ 5. Did you place your edited rough draft in your Rough Draft folder?

REVISING CHECK

_____ 6. Did you identify the purpose, type of writing, and audience?

_____ 7. Did you check for a topic, topic sentence, and sentences supporting the topic?

_____ 8. Did you check sentences for the right order, and did you combine, rearrange, or delete sentences when necessary?

_____ 9. Did you check for a variety of simple and compound sentences?

_____ 10. Did you check for any left out, repeated, or unnecessary words?

_____ 11. Did you check for the best choice of words by replacing or deleting unclear words?

_____ 12. Did you check the content for interest and creativity?

_____ 13. Did you check the voice to make sure the writing says what you want it to say?

EDITING CHECK

_____ 14. Did you indent each paragraph?

_____ 15. Did you circle each error and write corrections above it?

_____ 16. Did you capitalize the first word and put an end mark at the end of every sentence?

_____ 17. Did you check for all other capitalization mistakes?

_____ 18. Did you check for all punctuation mistakes?
(*commas, periods, apostrophes, quotation marks, underlining*)

_____ 19. Did you check for misspelled words and for incorrect homonym choices?

_____ 20. Did you check for incorrect spellings of plural and possessive forms?

_____ 21. Did you check for correct construction and punctuation of your sentences?

_____ 22. Did you check for usage mistakes? (*subject/verb agreement, a/an choices, contractions, verb tenses, degrees of adjectives, double negatives*)

_____ 23. Did you put your revised and edited paper in the Rough Draft folder?

FINAL PAPER CHECK

_____ 24. Did you write the final paper in pencil?

_____ 25. Did you center the title on the top line and center your name under the title?

_____ 26. Did you skip a line before starting the writing assignment?

_____ 27. Did you single-space, use wide margins, and write the final paper neatly?

_____ 28. Did you staple your papers in this order: final paper on top, rough draft in the middle, and prewriting map on the bottom? Did you put them in the Final Paper folder?

SHURLEY ENGLISH

Notes: _____

_____

_____

_____

_____

_____

_____

_____

_____

_____

_____

_____

_____

_____

_____

_____

_____

_____

_____

_____

_____

_____

_____

_____

_____

_____

Classroom Practice 47

Name:_____ Date:_____

GRAMMAR

▶ **Exercise 1:** Classify each sentence.

1. _____ The cabdriver gave us a city map of Miami.

2. _____ Ron and Don made their mother a birthday card.

3. _____ Sandra's teacher told her the answer to the problem.

▶ **Exercise 2:** Use Sentence 3 above to complete the table below.

List the Noun Used	List the Noun Job	Singular or Plural	Common or Proper	Simple Subject	Simple Predicate

SKILLS

▶ **Exercise 3:** For each noun, write the rule number and the plural form that follows the rule. Some nouns have two acceptable plural forms, but you should use the plural spellings that can be verified by these rules.

RULES FOR MAKING REGULAR NOUNS PLURAL
Add -s to nouns without special endings.
  1. most singular nouns.
Add -es to nouns with these special endings:
  2. *ch, sh, z, s, ss, x*.
  3. a consonant plus *y*, change *y* to *i* before adding **es**.

Add -s to nouns with this special ending:
4. a vowel plus *y*.

RULES FOR MAKING IRREGULAR NOUNS PLURAL
5. Change the spelling completely
  for the plural form.

	Rule	Plural Form		Rule	Plural Form
1. baby			6. pony		
2. truck			7. mouse		
3. man			8. guppy		
4. key			9. bench		
5. bush			10. bus		

EDITING

▶ **Exercise 4:** Put punctuation corrections within the sentence. Write all other corrections above the sentence.
Editing Guide: End Marks: 4   Capitals: 4   Commas: 2   Singular Words to Plural Words: 6

our family reunion was a great success the man visited with each other the woman took

care of baby and talked the child ate home-grown peach rode gentle pony and had a great day

Notes: _____

Classroom Practice 48

Name:_____ Date:_____

GRAMMAR

▶ **Exercise 1:** Classify each sentence.

1. _____ The salesman sold his customer an expensive boat.

2. _____ The captain gave his men a simple command.

3. _____ Tony peeled his little brother an orange.

▶ **Exercise 2:** Use Sentence 3 above to complete the table below.

List the Noun Used	List the Noun Job	Singular or Plural	Common or Proper	Simple Subject	Simple Predicate

SKILLS

▶ **Exercise 3:** For each noun, write the rule number and the plural form that follows the rule. Some nouns have two acceptable plural forms, but you should use the plural spellings that can be verified by these rules.

RULES FOR MAKING REGULAR NOUNS PLURAL
Add -s to nouns without special endings.
  1. most singular nouns.
Add -es to nouns with these special endings:
  2. *ch, sh, z, s, ss, x.*
  3. a consonant plus *y*, change *y* to *i* before adding **es**.

Add -s to nouns with this special ending:
  4. a vowel plus *y*.

RULES FOR MAKING IRREGULAR NOUNS PLURAL
  5. Change the spelling completely for the plural form.

	Rule	Plural Form		Rule	Plural Form
1. cup			6. sister		
2. fly			7. puppy		
3. dress			8. child		
4. goose			9. chimney		
5. foot			10. torch		

EDITING

▶ **Exercise 4:** Put punctuation corrections within the sentence. Write all other corrections above the sentence.
  Editing Guide: End Marks: 4 Capitals: 4 Commas: 1 Homonyms: 2 Singular Words to Plural Words: 4

we watched the goose fly over our house today you could here them quite plainly we saw

gray goose but we did not sea a white one our two little puppy barked loudly at all the goose

Notes: _____

Classroom Practice 49

Name:_____ Date:_____

GRAMMAR

▶ **Exercise 1:** Classify each sentence.

1. _____ Today, Mama bought us new supplies for school.

2. _____ The teacher gave Sally and Amy extra math problems.

3. _____ Leave me the keys to your car.

▶ **Exercise 2:** Use Sentence 1 above to complete the table below.

List the Noun Used	List the Noun Job	Singular or Plural	Common or Proper	Simple Subject	Simple Predicate

SKILLS

▶ **Exercise 3:** For each noun, write the rule number and the plural form that follows the rule. Some nouns have two acceptable plural forms, but you should use the plural spellings that can be verified by these rules.

RULES FOR MAKING REGULAR NOUNS PLURAL
Add -s to nouns without special endings.
  1. most singular nouns.
Add -es to nouns with these special endings:
  2. *ch, sh, z, s, ss, x*.
  3. a consonant plus *y*, change *y* to *i* before adding **es**.

Add -s to nouns with this special ending:
  4. a vowel plus *y*.

RULES FOR MAKING IRREGULAR NOUNS PLURAL
  5. Change the spelling completely
    for the plural form.

	Rule	Plural Form		Rule	Plural Form
1. class			6. lamp		
2. barn			7. patch		
3. daisy			8. pulley		
4. monkey			9. gentleman		
5. tooth			10. lobby		

EDITING

▶ **Exercise 4:** Put punctuation corrections within the sentence. Write all other corrections above the sentence.
  Editing Guide: End Marks: 4 Capitals: 4 Commas: 1 Apostrophes: 1 Singular Words to Plural Words: 2

the dentist cleaned my tooth today he covered my eyes with two black patch and played pirate

music he was quite a gentleman and he gave me a CD of pirate music i cant wait to go back

Notes: _____

_____

_____

_____

_____

_____

_____

_____

_____

_____

_____

_____

_____

_____

_____

_____

_____

_____

_____

_____

_____

_____

_____

_____

_____

_____

_____

_____

_____

_____

_____

Homework 8

On notebook paper, number 1–14. For each noun, write the rule number and the plural form that follows the rule. If a noun has two acceptable plural forms, use the plural spelling that can be verified by these rules.

RULES FOR MAKING REGULAR NOUNS PLURAL

Add -s to nouns without special endings.
1. most singular nouns.

Add -es to nouns with these special endings:
2. *ch, sh, z, s, ss, x.*
3. a consonant plus *y*, change *y* to *i* before adding **es**.

Add -s to nouns with this special ending:
4. a vowel plus **y**.

RULES FOR MAKING IRREGULAR NOUNS PLURAL
5. Change the spelling completely for the plural form.

	Rule	Plural Form		Rule	Plural Form
1. game			8. rabbit		
2. fox			9. valley		
3. berry			10. fireman		
4. boy			11. wish		
5. woman			12. cowboy		
6. city			13. grass		
7. boss			14. story		

Home Connection

Family Activity for Vocabulary and Analogies

Divide into family teams. The first team will use vocabulary and analogy cards 12–15 to ask questions about the information on their cards. The second team will use vocabulary and analogy cards 16–19 to ask questions about the information on their cards.

Family Activity for Plurals of Nouns

Write the plurals of the nouns in the blanks. Then, circle them in the word search below. Words may appear across or down.

lock _____

fly _____

toy _____

latch _____

man _____

cherry _____

pulley _____

scissors _____

sheep _____

tooth _____

```
Q E R H Y G H C P M S W A U V
W X F J A S D C P T E E T H S
O J S W I N S I T U M P E E F
Z K C O Q D F U A T D W E P O
F U I G P U L L E Y S Q A O T
P O S E L R E C O V Z C A O Q
L A S R U Y E E L O C K S F S
H T O Y S S G E A C G Z S E Z
L O R F E S O I T A P S H S R
D B S T T E N U C T S H E I L
S R E O T A B R H T F S E M A
Z G S Q I F L I E S H O P E P
E S H E R I F F S O E S D N N
C H E R R I E S N G A T S O R
```

Puzzle Answers: lock/locks fly/flies toy/toys latch/latches man/men cherry/cherries pulley/pulleys scissors/scissors sheep/sheep tooth/teeth

Student Workbook   Level 3   **119**

Notes: _____

_____

_____

_____

_____

_____

_____

_____

_____

_____

_____

_____

_____

_____

_____

_____

_____

_____

_____

_____

_____

_____

_____

_____

_____

_____

Chapter 10 Checkup 50

Name:_____ Date:_____

GRAMMAR

▶ **Exercise 1:** Classify each sentence.

1. _____ Yesterday, Wade handed Carla a surprise package.

2. _____ An artist on the coast gave Laura a beautiful painting.

3. _____ Pass me the salt and pepper.

▶ **Exercise 2:** Use Sentence 2 above to complete the table below.

List the Noun Used	List the Noun Job	Singular or Plural	Common or Proper	Simple Subject	Simple Predicate

SKILLS

▶ **Exercise 3:** For each noun, write the rule number and the plural form that follows the rule. Some nouns have two acceptable plural forms, but you should use the plural spellings that can be verified by these rules.

RULES FOR MAKING REGULAR NOUNS PLURAL
Add -s to nouns without special endings.
   1. most singular nouns.
Add -es to nouns with these special endings:
   2. *ch, sh, z, s, ss, x.*
   3. a consonant plus **y**, change **y** to **i** before adding **es**.

Add -s to nouns with this special ending:
   4. a vowel plus **y**.
RULES FOR MAKING IRREGULAR NOUNS PLURAL
   5. Change the spelling completely for the plural form.

	Rule	Plural Form			Rule	Plural Form
1. clock				6. father		
2. alley				7. bunch		
3. mouse				8. woman		
4. church				9. play		
5. tray				10. mystery		

EDITING

▶ **Exercise 4:** Put punctuation corrections within the sentence. Write all other corrections above the sentence.
   Editing Guide: End Marks: 4   Capitals: 6   Commas: 2   Homonyms: 1   Singular Words to Plural Words: 4

my friend and i love reading mystery books most man and woman read mysteries as child

i enjoy going too the library and i always check out a mystery book do you like mystery too

Notes: _____

_____

_____

_____

_____

_____

_____

_____

_____

_____

_____

_____

_____

_____

_____

_____

_____

_____

_____

_____

_____

_____

_____

_____

_____

_____

_____

_____

Classroom Practice 51

Name: _____ Date: _____

INDEPENDENT PRACTICE & REVISED SENTENCES

1. Write a Practice Sentence according to the labels you choose.
   Use **SN/SP V-t DO** as your main labels. You may use the other labels in any order and as many times as you wish in order to make a Practice Sentence.
   Chapter 10 labels for a Practice Sentence: SN/SP, V-t, IO, DO, Adj, Adv, A, P, OP, PPA, C, HV, I, PNA

2. Write a Revised Sentence. Use the following revision strategies: *synonym (syn), antonym (ant), word change (wc), added word (add), deleted word (delete),* or *no change (nc).* Under each word, write the abbreviation of the revision strategy you use.

Labels:

Practice:

Revised:

Strategies:

Labels:

Practice:

Revised:

Strategies:

Labels:

Practice:

Revised:

Strategies:

Notes: _____

_____

_____

_____

_____

_____

_____

_____

_____

_____

_____

_____

_____

_____

_____

_____

_____

_____

_____

_____

_____

_____

_____

_____

_____

_____

_____

_____

_____

_____

Chapter 10 Writing Evaluation Guide

Name:_____ Date:_____

ROUGH DRAFT CHECK

_____ 1. Did you write your rough draft in pencil?

_____ 2. Did you write the correct headings on the first seven lines of your paper?

_____ 3. Did you use extra wide margins and skip every other line?

_____ 4. Did you write a title at the end of your rough draft?

_____ 5. Did you place your edited rough draft in your Rough Draft folder?

REVISING CHECK

_____ 6. Did you identify the purpose, type of writing, and audience?

_____ 7. Did you check for a topic, topic sentence, and sentences supporting the topic?

_____ 8. Did you check sentences for the right order, and did you combine, rearrange, or delete sentences when necessary?

_____ 9. Did you check for a variety of simple and compound sentences?

_____ 10. Did you check for any left out, repeated, or unnecessary words?

_____ 11. Did you check for the best choice of words by replacing or deleting unclear words?

_____ 12. Did you check the content for interest and creativity?

_____ 13. Did you check the voice to make sure the writing says what you want it to say?

EDITING CHECK

_____ 14. Did you indent each paragraph?

_____ 15. Did you circle each error and write corrections above it?

_____ 16. Did you capitalize the first word and put an end mark at the end of every sentence?

_____ 17. Did you check for all other capitalization mistakes?

_____ 18. Did you check for all punctuation mistakes?
(commas, periods, apostrophes, quotation marks, underlining)

_____ 19. Did you check for misspelled words and for incorrect homonym choices?

_____ 20. Did you check for incorrect spellings of plural and possessive forms?

_____ 21. Did you check for correct construction and punctuation of your sentences?

_____ 22. Did you check for usage mistakes? *(subject/verb agreement, a/an choices, contractions, verb tenses, degrees of adjectives, double negatives)*

_____ 23. Did you put your revised and edited paper in the Rough Draft folder?

FINAL PAPER CHECK

_____ 24. Did you write the final paper in pencil?

_____ 25. Did you center the title on the top line and center your name under the title?

_____ 26. Did you skip a line before starting the writing assignment?

_____ 27. Did you single-space, use wide margins, and write the final paper neatly?

_____ 28. Did you staple your papers in this order: final paper on top, rough draft in the middle, and prewriting map on the bottom? Did you put them in the Final Paper folder?

Notes: _____

_____

_____

_____

_____

_____

_____

_____

_____

_____

_____

_____

_____

_____

_____

_____

_____

_____

_____

_____

_____

_____

_____

_____

_____

_____

_____

_____

_____

Classroom Practice 52

Name:_____ Date:_____

GRAMMAR

▶ **Exercise 1:** Classify each sentence.

1. _____ Thad and I rode a camel across the desert in the heat of summer.

2. _____ Our family flew to Grandma's house in California.

3. _____ Uncle Brad bought me a new DVD.

SKILLS & EDITING 1

▶ **Exercise 2:** Edit the sentences and underline the explanatory words. Use the Editing Guide below.

   (1.) 7 mistakes (2.) 7 mistakes (3.) 8 mistakes

1. i like pizza said molly

2. my dog had five puppies mary exclaimed happily

3. kelly can you spend the night asked shelby

SKILLS & EDITING 2

▶ **Exercise 3:** Edit the sentences and underline the explanatory words. Use the Editing Guide below.

   (1.) 8 mistakes (2.) 13 mistakes (3.) 7 mistakes

1. did you call the dentists office today mom asked

2. stephen we are going to grandmas house in dallas texas i whispered

3. dad we won the game shouted my brother loudly

SHURLEY ENGLISH

Notes: _____

_____

_____

_____

_____

_____

_____

_____

_____

_____

_____

_____

_____

_____

_____

_____

_____

_____

_____

_____

_____

_____

_____

_____

_____

_____

_____

_____

Classroom Practice 53

Name:_____ Date:_____

GRAMMAR

▶ **Exercise 1:** Classify each sentence.

1. _____ Yesterday, my aunt and uncle moved into a new apartment.

2. _____ She carried a red and green banner during the holiday parade.

3. _____ Bring me several cans of vegetables from the cabinet.

SKILLS & EDITING 1

▶ **Exercise 2:** Edit the sentences and underline the explanatory words. Use the Editing Guide below.
    (1.) 10 mistakes   (2.) 11 mistakes   (3.) 11 mistakes

1. kim said the birthday party is at marias house on saturday

2. mr miller asked did you speak spanish while you were in mexico

3. the tv announcer exclaimed take cover a tornado is headed your way

SKILLS & EDITING 2

▶ **Exercise 3:** Edit the sentences and underline the explanatory words. Use the Editing Guide below.
    (1.) 9 mistakes   (2.) 10 mistakes   (3.) 10 mistakes   (4.) 10 mistakes

1. dad may i be excused from the table asked danny

2. danny asked may i be excused from the table dad

3. cindy said ill call wednesday to make a doctors appointment

4. ill call wednesday to make a doctors appointment said cindy

Notes: _____

_____

_____

_____

_____

_____

_____

_____

_____

_____

_____

_____

_____

_____

_____

_____

_____

_____

_____

_____

_____

_____

_____

_____

_____

_____

_____

_____

_____

Classroom Practice 54

Name:_____ Date:_____

GRAMMAR

▶ **Exercise 1:** Classify each sentence.

1. _____ Hand the winner of the contest his prize.

2. _____ Dan's hat and coat hung on a hook by the door.

3. _____ Has Dana loaned you a book about jungle animals?

SKILLS & EDITING 1

▶ **Exercise 2:** Edit the sentences and underline the explanatory words. Use the Editing Guide below.

   (1.) 8 mistakes (2.) 9 mistakes (3.) 7 mistakes (4.) 7 mistakes

1. dan this is a great party exclaimed david

2. david exclaimed this is a great party dan

3. susan asked will you help me with this problem

4. will you help me with this problem asked susan

SKILLS & EDITING 2

▶ **Exercise 3:** Edit the sentences and underline the explanatory words. Use the Editing Guide below.

   (1.) 7 mistakes (2.) 8 mistakes (3.) 7 mistakes

1. sherry asked did you enjoy the movie

2. ill call you tomorrow said mike

3. andrew shouted lunch is ready

Notes: _____

_____

_____

_____

_____

_____

_____

_____

_____

_____

_____

_____

_____

_____

_____

_____

_____

_____

_____

_____

_____

_____

_____

_____

_____

_____

_____

_____

Classroom Practice 55

Name:_____ Date:_____

GRAMMAR

▶ **Exercise 1:** Classify each sentence.

1. _____ Kay and John are training several horses for us.

2. _____ William taught his puppy several new tricks.

3. _____ The baby's bottle fell noisily to the floor.

SKILLS & EDITING 1

▶ **Exercise 2:** Edit the sentences and underline the explanatory words. Use the Editing Guide below.

   (1.) 9 mistakes   (2.) 9 mistakes   (3.) 7 mistakes   (4.) 6 mistakes

1. yes i want to go shopping with you sharon answered

2. sharon answered yes i want to go shopping with you

3. my sister shouted your room is a mess

4. your room is a mess shouted my sister

SKILLS & EDITING 2

▶ **Exercise 3:** Edit the sentences and underline the explanatory words. Use the Editing Guide below.

   (1.) 9 mistakes   (2.) 7 mistakes   (3.) 9 mistakes

1. debbie asked do you like my new coat sara

2. we will go to the library at noon said johnny

3. clay and trey shouted its snowing outside

SHURLEY ENGLISH

Notes: _____

_____

_____

_____

_____

_____

_____

_____

_____

_____

_____

_____

_____

_____

_____

_____

_____

_____

_____

_____

_____

_____

_____

_____

_____

_____

_____

_____

Chapter 11 Checkup 56

Name:_____ Date:_____

GRAMMAR

▶ **Exercise 1:** Classify each sentence.

1. _____ Look! A little brown rabbit is munching clover in our backyard!

2. _____ I will write your teacher a note for your absence.

3. _____ The steamboat floated lazily down the muddy river.

SKILLS & EDITING 1

▶ **Exercise 2:** Edit the sentences and underline the explanatory words. Use the Editing Guide below.

(1.) 9 mistakes   (2.) 10 mistakes   (3.) 9 mistakes   (4.) 8 mistakes

1. roger   would   you   like   more   pie   asked   aunt   ruth

2. aunt   ruth   asked   would   you   like   more   pie   roger

3. julie   exclaimed   my   yellow   cat   just   had   five   kittens   darrell

4. darrell   my   yellow   cat   just   had   five   kittens   exclaimed   julie

SKILLS & EDITING 2

▶ **Exercise 3:** Edit the sentences and underline the explanatory words. Use the Editing Guide below.

(1.) 9 mistakes   (2.) 12 mistakes   (3.) 9 mistakes

1. uncle   bob   do   you   like   to   go   fishing   asked   randy

2. uncle   bob   replied   yes   i   like   to   go   fishing   it   is   my   favorite   sport

3. randy   said   i   am   really   glad   to   hear   that   do   you   want   to   go   fishing   with   me   tomorrow

Notes: _____

_____

_____

_____

_____

_____

_____

_____

_____

_____

_____

_____

_____

_____

_____

_____

_____

_____

_____

_____

_____

_____

_____

_____

_____

_____

_____

_____

_____

_____

_____

Chapter 11 Writing Evaluation Guide

Name: _____ Date: _____

ROUGH DRAFT CHECK

_____ 1. Did you write your rough draft in pencil?

_____ 2. Did you write the correct headings on the first seven lines of your paper?

_____ 3. Did you use extra wide margins and skip every other line?

_____ 4. Did you write a title at the end of your rough draft?

_____ 5. Did you place your edited rough draft in your Rough Draft folder?

REVISING CHECK

_____ 6. Did you identify the purpose, type of writing, and audience?

_____ 7. Did you check for a topic, topic sentence, and sentences supporting the topic?

_____ 8. Did you check sentences for the right order, and did you combine, rearrange, or delete sentences when necessary?

_____ 9. Did you check for a variety of simple and compound sentences?

_____ 10. Did you check for any left out, repeated, or unnecessary words?

_____ 11. Did you check for the best choice of words by replacing or deleting unclear words?

_____ 12. Did you check the content for interest and creativity?

_____ 13. Did you check the voice to make sure the writing says what you want it to say?

EDITING CHECK

_____ 14. Did you indent each paragraph?

_____ 15. Did you circle each error and write corrections above it?

_____ 16. Did you capitalize the first word and put an end mark at the end of every sentence?

_____ 17. Did you check for all other capitalization mistakes?

_____ 18. Did you check for all punctuation mistakes? *(commas, periods, apostrophes, quotation marks, underlining)*

_____ 19. Did you check for misspelled words and for incorrect homonym choices?

_____ 20. Did you check for incorrect spellings of plural and possessive forms?

_____ 21. Did you check for correct construction and punctuation of your sentences?

_____ 22. Did you check for usage mistakes? *(subject/verb agreement, a/an choices, contractions, verb tenses, degrees of adjectives, double negatives)*

_____ 23. Did you put your revised and edited paper in the Rough Draft folder?

FINAL PAPER CHECK

_____ 24. Did you write the final paper in pencil?

_____ 25. Did you center the title on the top line and center your name under the title?

_____ 26. Did you skip a line before starting the writing assignment?

_____ 27. Did you single-space, use wide margins, and write the final paper neatly?

_____ 28. Did you staple your papers in this order: final paper on top, rough draft in the middle, and prewriting map on the bottom? Did you put them in the Final Paper folder?

SHURLEY ENGLISH

Notes: _____

_____

_____

_____

_____

_____

_____

_____

_____

_____

_____

_____

_____

_____

_____

_____

_____

_____

_____

_____

_____

_____

_____

_____

_____

_____

_____

Classroom Practice 57

Name:_____ Date:_____

GRAMMAR

▶ **Exercise 1:** Classify each sentence.

1. _____ A fire damaged my father's new store.

2. _____ Aunt Bee made me a costume for the school play.

3. _____ Have the students studied for their spelling test?

▶ **Exercise 2:** Use Sentence 2 above to complete the table below.

List the Noun Used	List the Noun Job	Singular or Plural	Common or Proper	Simple Subject	Simple Predicate

SKILLS

▶ **Exercise 3:** Complete the table below.
Use these patterns. **SN V   SN V-t DO   SN V-t IO DO   SN LV PrN   SN LV PA**

Underline the Subject and the Verb.	Write the pattern.	Write the verb.	Write LV or AV.
1. Dad gave us a present.			
2. Butterflies are pretty.			
3. Missy was a helper at the zoo.			
4. Jacob worked on his model car.			
5. Brent saw four planes in the sky.			

EDITING

▶ **Exercise 4:** Edit the Jason and Sally story, "The Mouse." (Part 1 of 6)
Editing Guide: (1.) 7 mistakes   (2.) 7 mistakes

1. i cant find my pet mouse moaned jason as he turned everything in his room upside down

2. sally stuck her head in his room and said you better find that mouse before mom gets home

Notes: _____

_____

_____

_____

_____

_____

_____

_____

_____

_____

_____

_____

_____

_____

_____

_____

_____

_____

_____

_____

_____

_____

_____

_____

_____

_____

_____

_____

_____

_____

_____

Classroom Practice 58

Name:_____ Date:_____

GRAMMAR

▶ **Exercise 1:** Classify each sentence.

1. _____ The small donkey carried a huge load.

2. _____ Patty left her mother a note from her teacher.

3. _____ Geese fly south for the winter.

SKILLS

▶ **Exercise 2:** Complete the table below.
Use these patterns. **SN V   SN V-t DO   SN V-t IO DO   SN LV PrN   SN LV PA**

Underline the <u>Subject</u> and the <u>Verb</u>.	Write the pattern.	Write the verb.	Write LV or AV.
1. My new dress is a dark purple.			
2. Jan walked to the park.			
3. Jay was the leader of their band.			
4. Dana brought chips for our picnic.			
5. Grandpa gave me a ride.			

▶ **Exercise 3:** Underline the negative words in each sentence. Rewrite each sentence and correct the double-negative mistake as indicated by the rule number in parentheses at the end of the sentence.

RULE 1:	RULE 2:	RULE 3:
Change the second negative to a positive.	**Take out the negative part of a contraction.**	**Remove the first negative word (verb change).**

1. We never go nowhere.   **(Rule 1)** _____

2. Sandy couldn't carry nothing heavy. **(Rule 1)** _____

3. Seth hasn't never been to the park. **(Rule 2)** _____

4. We don't have no tests today.   **(Rule 3)** _____

EDITING

▶ **Exercise 4:** Edit the Jason and Sally story, "The Mouse." (Part 2 of 6)
Editing Guide: (1.) 7 mistakes   (2.) 8 mistakes

1. sally could you help me find my mouse jason asked his sister in desperation

2. sally thought for a minute and then said what do i get if i help you

SHURLEY ENGLISH

Notes: _____

_____

_____

_____

_____

_____

_____

_____

_____

_____

_____

_____

_____

_____

_____

_____

_____

_____

_____

_____

_____

_____

_____

_____

_____

_____

_____

_____

Classroom Practice 59

Name:_____ Date:_____

GRAMMAR

▶ **Exercise 1:** Classify each sentence.

1. _____ The old gentleman gave the taxi driver a huge tip.

2. _____ Did Jill buy her lunch at the art museum?

3. _____ Yea! Our team won!

SKILLS

▶ **Exercise 2:** Complete the table below.
Use these patterns. **SN V   SN V-t DO   SN V-t IO DO   SN LV PrN   SN LV PA**

Underline the Subject and the Verb.	Write the pattern.	Write the verb.	Write LV or AV.
1. Shelly wrote a poem for her dad.			
2. These bananas are rotten.			
3. He works in that restaurant.			
4. Sam gave Larry a frog.			
5. My mother is a nurse.			

▶ **Exercise 3:** Underline the negative words in each sentence. Rewrite each sentence and correct the double-negative mistake as indicated by the rule number in parentheses at the end of the sentence.

RULE 1:	RULE 2:	RULE 3:
Change the second negative to a positive.	Take out the negative part of a contraction.	Remove the first negative word (verb change).

1. There isn't no more cake.   **(Rule 2)** _____

2. Cindy never wants nothing for lunch. **(Rule 1)** _____

3. We don't have no money.   **(Rule 3)** _____

4. Wesley hasn't never played with us. **(Rule 2)** _____

EDITING

▶ **Exercise 4:** Edit the Jason and Sally story, "The Mouse." (Part 3 of 6)
Editing Guide: (1.) 9 mistakes   (2.) 10 mistakes

1. well you could feel good about saving me from mothers list jason said

2. sally laughed and said you stay on mothers list all the time and i feel pretty good right now

Notes: _____

_____

_____

_____

_____

_____

_____

_____

_____

_____

_____

_____

_____

_____

_____

_____

_____

_____

_____

_____

_____

_____

_____

_____

_____

_____

_____

_____

Classroom Practice 60

Name:_____ Date:_____

GRAMMAR

▶ **Exercise 1:** Classify each sentence.

1. _____ I want a crisp salad with tomatoes for lunch today.

2. _____ Our music teacher taught us a new song.

3. _____ Blackberries and blueberries grow on bushes.

SKILLS

▶ **Exercise 2:** Complete the table below.
Use these patterns. **SN V   SN V-t DO   SN V-t IO DO   SN LV PrN   SN LV PA**

Underline the Subject and the Verb.	Write the pattern.	Write the verb.	Write LV or AV.
1. Amber read Kelly a story.			
2. Jerry fixed my computer.			
3. The clowns are very funny.			
4. Trey is a detective.			
5. Judy fell in the mud.			

▶ **Exercise 3:** Underline the negative words in each sentence. Rewrite each sentence and correct the double-negative mistake as indicated by the rule number in parentheses at the end of the sentence.

RULE 1:	RULE 2:	RULE 3:
Change the second negative to a positive.	**Take out the negative part of a contraction.**	**Remove the first negative word (verb change).**

1. They don't have no syrup. **(Rule3)** _____

2. Sarah never heard nothing. **(Rule 1)** _____

3. We didn't sell nobody a ticket. **(Rule 1)** _____

4. I won't have no homework today. **(Rule 2)** _____

EDITING

▶ **Exercise 4:** Edit the Jason and Sally story, "The Mouse." (Part 4 of 6)
Editing Guide: (1.) 6 mistakes   (2.) 10 mistakes

1. you could feel even better if you helped me find my pet mouse jason said

2. sally replied youll have to do better than that and you had better hurry mom just got home

Notes: _____

_____

_____

_____

_____

_____

_____

_____

_____

_____

_____

_____

_____

_____

_____

_____

_____

_____

_____

_____

_____

_____

_____

_____

_____

_____

Chapter 12 Checkup 61

Name:_____ Date:_____

GRAMMAR

▶ **Exercise 1:** Classify each sentence.

1. _____ Larry builds and repairs lawnmowers for his family and friends.

2. _____ Did you mail Tim and Hope an invitation?

3. _____ The boys and girls are listening carefully to your instructions.

SKILLS

▶ **Exercise 2:** Complete the table below. **SN V   SN V-t DO   SN V-t IO DO   SN LV PrN   SN LV PA**

Underline the <u>Subject</u> and the <u>Verb</u>.	Write the pattern.	Write the verb.	Write LV or AV.
1. Randy repaired the telephone.			
2. Whales are mammals.			
3. Sheri stayed home.			
4. The pies are delicious.			
5. Nana gave the baby a bottle.			

▶ **Exercise 3:** Underline the negative words in each sentence. Rewrite each sentence and correct the double-negative mistake as indicated by the rule number in parentheses at the end of the sentence.

RULE 1:	RULE 2:	RULE 3:
Change the second negative to a positive.	Take out the negative part of a contraction.	Remove the first negative word (verb change).

1. There isn't no medicine here.   (Rule 2) _____

2. I can't hardly wait for the concert.   (Rule 2) _____

3. He hasn't done nothing today.   (Rule 1)_____

4. Jason didn't say nothing.   (Rule 3) _____

EDITING

▶ **Exercise 4:** Punctuate the Jason and Sally story, "The Mouse." (Part 5 of 6)

 Editing Guide: (1.) 11 mistakes   (2.) 11 mistakes

1. you win jason said quickly as he heard his mom in the hall ill do your dish chores for a week

2. sally smiled youll find your mouse in his cage i found him in my room earlier and i put him back

SHURLEY ENGLISH

Notes: _____

_____

_____

_____

_____

_____

_____

_____

_____

_____

_____

_____

_____

_____

_____

_____

_____

_____

_____

_____

_____

_____

_____

_____

_____

_____

_____

_____

Chapter 12 Writing Evaluation Guide

Name:_____ Date:_____

ROUGH DRAFT CHECK

_____ 1. Did you write your rough draft in pencil?

_____ 2. Did you write the correct headings on the first seven lines of your paper?

_____ 3. Did you use extra wide margins and skip every other line?

_____ 4. Did you write a title at the end of your rough draft?

_____ 5. Did you place your edited rough draft in your Rough Draft folder?

REVISING CHECK

_____ 6. Did you identify the purpose, type of writing, and audience?

_____ 7. Did you check for a topic, topic sentence, and sentences supporting the topic?

_____ 8. Did you check sentences for the right order, and did you combine, rearrange, or delete sentences when necessary?

_____ 9. Did you check for a variety of simple and compound sentences?

_____ 10. Did you check for any left out, repeated, or unnecessary words?

_____ 11. Did you check for the best choice of words by replacing or deleting unclear words?

_____ 12. Did you check the content for interest and creativity?

_____ 13. Did you check the voice to make sure the writing says what you want it to say?

EDITING CHECK

_____ 14. Did you indent each paragraph?

_____ 15. Did you circle each error and write corrections above it?

_____ 16. Did you capitalize the first word and put an end mark at the end of every sentence?

_____ 17. Did you check for all other capitalization mistakes?

_____ 18. Did you check for all punctuation mistakes?
(commas, periods, apostrophes, quotation marks, underlining)

_____ 19. Did you check for misspelled words and for incorrect homonym choices?

_____ 20. Did you check for incorrect spellings of plural and possessive forms?

_____ 21. Did you check for correct construction and punctuation of your sentences?

_____ 22. Did you check for usage mistakes? (subject/verb agreement, a/an choices, contractions, verb tenses, degrees of adjectives, double negatives)

_____ 23. Did you put your revised and edited paper in the Rough Draft folder?

FINAL PAPER CHECK

_____ 24. Did you write the final paper in pencil?

_____ 25. Did you center the title on the top line and center your name under the title?

_____ 26. Did you skip a line before starting the writing assignment?

_____ 27. Did you single-space, use wide margins, and write the final paper neatly?

_____ 28. Did you staple your papers in this order: final paper on top, rough draft in the middle, and prewriting map on the bottom? Did you put them in the Final Paper folder?

SHURLEY ENGLISH

Notes: _____

_____

_____

_____

_____

_____

_____

_____

_____

_____

_____

_____

_____

_____

_____

_____

_____

_____

_____

_____

_____

_____

_____

_____

_____

Classroom Practice 62

Name:_____ Date:_____

GRAMMAR

▶ **Exercise 1:** Classify each sentence.

1. _____ Several math books fell on the floor yesterday.

2. _____ Have you finished your homework tonight?

3. _____ I fed the pretty brown pony an apple today.

▶ **Exercise 2:** Use Sentence 3 above to complete the table below.

List the Noun Used	List the Noun Job	Singular or Plural	Common or Proper	Simple Subject	Simple Predicate

SKILLS

▶ **Exercise 3: For Part A,** underline each noun to be made possessive. Write **S** for singular or **P** for plural, the rule number, and the possessive form. **For Part B,** write the singular possessive and plural possessive of each noun.

RULE 1: boy's For a singular noun — add ('s)	**RULE 2: boys'** For a plural noun that ends in s — add (')	**RULE 3: men's** For a plural noun that does not end in s — add ('s)

Part A	S-P	Rule	Possessive Form	Part B	Singular Poss	Plural Poss
1. cars tires				7. sister		
2. cat paw				8. dress		
3. James key				9. foot		
4. boy bed				10. bike		
5. baby toy				11. shoe		
6. men gloves				12. child		

EDITING

▶ **Exercise 4:** Edit the sentence below and underline the explanatory words. **Editing Guide: 11 mistakes**

do you need someone to mow your yard asked george my prices are very reasonable

Notes: _____

_____

_____

_____

_____

_____

_____

_____

_____

_____

_____

_____

_____

_____

_____

_____

_____

_____

_____

_____

_____

_____

_____

_____

_____

_____

_____

_____

_____

_____

Classroom Practice 63

Name:_____ Date:_____

GRAMMAR

▶ **Exercise 1:** Classify each sentence.

1. _____ Several children played on the swings during recess.

2. _____ My sister bought me a new watch for my birthday.

3. _____ The referee blew his whistle loudly during the game.

▶ **Exercise 2:** Use Sentence 2 above to complete the table below.

List the Noun Used	List the Noun Job	Singular or Plural	Common or Proper	Simple Subject	Simple Predicate

SKILLS

▶ **Exercise 3: For Part A**, underline each noun to be made possessive. Write **S** for singular or **P** for plural, the rule number, and the possessive form. **For Part B**, write the singular possessive and plural possessive of each noun.

RULE 1: **boy's**	RULE 2: **boys'**	RULE 3: **men's**
For a singular noun — add ('s)	For a plural noun that ends in s — add (')	For a plural noun that does not end in s — add ('s)

Part A	S-P	Rule	Possessive Form	Part B	Singular Poss	Plural Poss
1. elves hats				7. class		
2. hero cape				8. man		
3. babies bottles				9. monkey		
4. book pages				10. mouse		
5. women jobs				11. soldier		
6. geese eggs				12. clown		

EDITING

▶ **Exercise 4:** Edit the sentence below and underline the explanatory words. **Editing Guide: 9 mistakes**

stanley said i would like two orders of fries a jumbo hamburger and an extra large drink

SHURLEY ENGLISH

Notes: _____

_____

_____

_____

_____

_____

_____

_____

_____

_____

_____

_____

_____

_____

_____

_____

_____

_____

_____

_____

_____

_____

_____

_____

_____

_____

_____

_____

Classroom Practice 64

Name:_____ Date:_____

GRAMMAR

▶ **Exercise 1:** Classify each sentence.

1. _____ The campers told us a wild story about bears.

2. _____ He wrote very carefully on his test paper.

3. _____ I have given that old coat and hat away.

▶ **Exercise 2:** Use Sentence 1 above to complete the table below.

List the Noun Used	List the Noun Job	Singular or Plural	Common or Proper	Simple Subject	Simple Predicate

SKILLS

▶ **Exercise 3: For Part A**, underline each noun to be made possessive. Write **S** for singular or **P** for plural, the rule number, and the possessive form. **For Part B**, write the singular possessive and plural possessive of each noun.

RULE 1: **boy's**	RULE 2: **boys'**	RULE 3: **men's**
For a singular noun — add ('s)	For a plural noun that ends in s — add (')	For a plural noun that does not end in s — add ('s)

Part A	S-P	Rule	Possessive Form	Part B	Singular Poss	Plural Poss
1. birds wings				6. mouse		
2. Tom hat				7. fly		
3. doctor office				8. boy		
4. teachers desks				9. ant		
5. children toys				10. man		

EDITING

▶ **Exercise 4:** Edit the sentence below and underline the explanatory words. **Editing Guide: 11 mistakes**

adam will you pick up travis and jason from their grandmothers house mom asked

Notes: _____

_____

_____

_____

_____

_____

_____

_____

_____

_____

_____

_____

_____

_____

_____

_____

_____

_____

_____

_____

_____

_____

_____

_____

_____

_____

_____

_____

_____

_____

Chapter 13 Checkup 65

Name:_____ Date:_____

GRAMMAR

▶ **Exercise 1:** Classify each sentence.

1. _____ Gee! That bold little mouse gave me a scare!

2. _____ A strong wind shook the shutters on our house!

3. _____ Are Justin and Holly going to the library today?

▶ **Exercise 2:** Use Sentence 3 above to complete the table below.

List the Noun Used	List the Noun Job	Singular or Plural	Common or Proper	Simple Subject	Simple Predicate

SKILLS

▶ **Exercise 3: For Part A**, underline each noun to be made possessive. Write **S** for singular or **P** for plural, the rule number, and the possessive form. **For Part B**, write the singular possessive and plural possessive of each noun.

RULE 1: boy's	RULE 2: boys'	RULE 3: men's
For a singular noun — add ('s)	For a plural noun that ends in s — add (')	For a plural noun that does not end in s — add ('s)

Part A	S-P	Rule	Possessive Form	Part B	Singular Poss	Plural Poss
1. shoes heels				6. tooth		
2. dad car				7. box		
3. Ryan bed				8. tomato		
4. girls bikes				9. baby		
5. sister jeans				10. mouse		

EDITING

▶ **Exercise 4:** Edit the sentence below and underline the explanatory words. **Editing Guide: 16 mistakes**

dad said our dogs abby coco and buddy are out of food would you get them some today

SHURLEY ENGLISH

Notes: _____

_____

_____

_____

_____

_____

_____

_____

_____

_____

_____

_____

_____

_____

_____

_____

_____

_____

_____

_____

_____

_____

_____

_____

_____

_____

_____

_____

_____

_____

Chapter 13 Writing Evaluation Guide

Name:_____ Date:_____

ROUGH DRAFT CHECK

_____ 1. Did you write your rough draft in pencil?

_____ 2. Did you write the correct headings on the first seven lines of your paper?

_____ 3. Did you use extra wide margins and skip every other line?

_____ 4. Did you write a title at the end of your rough draft?

_____ 5. Did you place your edited rough draft in your Rough Draft folder?

REVISING CHECK

_____ 6. Did you identify the purpose, type of writing, and audience?

_____ 7. Did you check for a topic, topic sentence, and sentences supporting the topic?

_____ 8. Did you check sentences for the right order, and did you combine, rearrange, or delete sentences when necessary?

_____ 9. Did you check for a variety of simple and compound sentences?

_____ 10. Did you check for any left out, repeated, or unnecessary words?

_____ 11. Did you check for the best choice of words by replacing or deleting unclear words?

_____ 12. Did you check the content for interest and creativity?

_____ 13. Did you check the voice to make sure the writing says what you want it to say?

EDITING CHECK

_____ 14. Did you indent each paragraph?

_____ 15. Did you circle each error and write corrections above it?

_____ 16. Did you capitalize the first word and put an end mark at the end of every sentence?

_____ 17. Did you check for all other capitalization mistakes?

_____ 18. Did you check for all punctuation mistakes?
(commas, periods, apostrophes, quotation marks, underlining)

_____ 19. Did you check for misspelled words and for incorrect homonym choices?

_____ 20. Did you check for incorrect spellings of plural and possessive forms?

_____ 21. Did you check for correct construction and punctuation of your sentences?

_____ 22. Did you check for usage mistakes? *(subject/verb agreement, a/an choices, contractions, verb tenses, degrees of adjectives, double negatives)*

_____ 23. Did you put your revised and edited paper in the Rough Draft folder?

FINAL PAPER CHECK

_____ 24. Did you write the final paper in pencil?

_____ 25. Did you center the title on the top line and center your name under the title?

_____ 26. Did you skip a line before starting the writing assignment?

_____ 27. Did you single-space, use wide margins, and write the final paper neatly?

_____ 28. Did you staple your papers in this order: final paper on top, rough draft in the middle, and prewriting map on the bottom? Did you put them in the Final Paper folder?

SHURLEY ENGLISH

Notes: _____

_____

_____

_____

_____

_____

_____

_____

_____

_____

_____

_____

_____

_____

_____

_____

_____

_____

_____

_____

_____

_____

_____

_____

_____

_____

_____

_____

_____

Classroom Practice 66

Name:_____ Date:_____

GRAMMAR

▶ **Exercise 1:** Classify each sentence.

1. _____ Dad drove the old truck along the edge of the pond.

2. _____ Did Brandon build a model airplane for his science project?

3. _____ Grandmother sent me a postcard from Alaska.

SKILLS

▶ **Exercise 2:** Write the different forms for the adjectives below.

RULE 1: Simple form	RULE 2: Comparative form (er, more)	RULE 3: Superlative form (est, most)

Simple Form	Comparative Form	Superlative Form
1. funny		
2. good		
3. interesting		
4. nice		
5. helpful		
6. bad		

▶ **Exercise 3:** In each blank, write the correct form of the adjective in parentheses to complete the sentences.

1. Our new car is _____than our old one. **(good)**

2. This trail is the _____trail on the mountain. **(difficult)**

3. Katherine was a very _____assistant. **(helpful)**

4. My throat hurts_____today than yesterday. **(bad)**

5. Greenwood has received _____rain than Glendale. **(little)**

EDITING

▶ **Exercise 4:** Edit the sentence below and underline the explanatory words. **Editing Guide: 9 mistakes**

who is going to the game with mom and dad asked shannon

SHURLEY ENGLISH

Notes: _____

_____

_____

_____

_____

_____

_____

_____

_____

_____

_____

_____

_____

_____

_____

_____

_____

_____

_____

_____

_____

_____

_____

_____

_____

_____

_____

_____

Classroom Practice 67

Name:_____ Date:_____

GRAMMAR

▶ **Exercise 1:** Classify each sentence.

1. _____ Bring two loaves of bread to the party.

2. _____ They are waiting patiently for the early bus.

3. _____ Yesterday, Darren showed the officer the broken window.

SKILLS

▶ **Exercise 2:** Write the different forms for the adjectives below.

| RULE 1: Simple form | RULE 2: Comparative form (er, more) | RULE 3: Superlative form (est, most) |

Simple Form	Comparative Form	Superlative Form
1. noisy		
2. unusual		
3. kind		
4. helpful		
5. good		
6. playful		
7. bad		

▶ **Exercise 3:** In each blank, write the correct form of the adjective in parentheses to complete the sentences.

1. A person's heart is_____than a dog's heart. **(large)**

2. Some cats are _____hunters than others. **(skillful)**

3. The hummingbird has the_____heart rate of any animal. **(fast)**

4. Jim is_____than I am. **(active)**

5. This is the _____weather of the whole week. **(bad)**

EDITING

▶ **Exercise 4:** Edit the sentence below and underline the explanatory words. **Editing Guide: 10 mistakes**

the fans shouted we want a touchdown pass the football to calvin

SHURLEY ENGLISH

Notes: _____

_____

_____

_____

_____

_____

_____

_____

_____

_____

_____

_____

_____

_____

_____

_____

_____

_____

_____

_____

_____

_____

_____

_____

_____

_____

_____

Classroom Practice 68

Name:_____ Date:_____

GRAMMAR

▶ **Exercise 1:** Classify each sentence.

1. _____ The chocolate candy did melt quickly in the hot car!

2. _____ He gave me a notebook and pen for my meeting.

3. _____ Today, she and I chased butterflies through a field of wildflowers.

SKILLS

▶ **Exercise 2:** Write the different forms for the adjectives below.

RULE 1: Simple form	RULE 2: Comparative form (er, more)	RULE 3: Superlative form (est, most)

Simple Form	Comparative Form	Superlative Form
1. tall		
2. useful		
3. safe		
4. curious		
5. good		
6. little		

▶ **Exercise 3:** In each blank, write the correct form of the adjective in parentheses to complete the sentences.

1. My uncle had a very _____ vacation. (**interesting**)

2. Today was the _____ day of this week. (**bad**)

3. He had the _____ painting of all. (**beautiful**)

4. Our house is _____ than our neighbor's house. (**valuable**)

5. I have _____ money now than I did yesterday. (**little**)

EDITING

▶ **Exercise 4:** Edit the sentence below and underline the explanatory words. **Editing Guide: 9 mistakes**

andy will you and todd wash the car today mom asked

Notes: _____

Chapter 14 Checkup 69

Name:_____ Date:_____

GRAMMAR

▶ **Exercise 1:** Classify each sentence.

1. _____ He told me his plans for summer vacation.

2. _____ Did your brother clean and organize his room yesterday?

3. _____ For several days, the campers cooked over an open fire.

SKILLS

▶ **Exercise 2:** Write the different forms for the adjectives below.

RULE 1: Simple form	RULE 2: Comparative form (er, more)	RULE 3: Superlative form (est, most)

Simple Form	Comparative Form	Superlative Form
1. good		
2. thin		
3. ripe		
4. excited		
5. close		
6. bad		

▶ **Exercise 3:** In each blank, write the correct form of the adjective in parentheses to complete the sentences.

1. Howard's project was _____ than mine. **(good)**

2. This tea is _____ than Mother's tea. **(sweet)**

3. My new puppy is the _____ pet I have ever had. **(lovable)**

4. This is the _____ day of the year. **(hot)**

5. This test was _____ than the last one. **(difficult)**

EDITING

▶ **Exercise 4:** Edit the sentence below and underline the explanatory words. **Editing Guide: 13 mistakes**

donald said i am going on a nature hike with matt kathy and carla on saturday

SHURLEY ENGLISH

Notes: _____

_____

_____

_____

_____

_____

_____

_____

_____

_____

_____

_____

_____

_____

_____

_____

_____

_____

_____

_____

_____

_____

_____

_____

_____

Classroom Practice 70

Name:_____ Date:_____

SKILLS

Use the title and letter parts below to fill in the blanks of the friendly letter.

TITLE PARTS of a Friendly Letter:

Closing   **Signature**   **Heading**

Greeting   **Body**

SAMPLE PARTS of a Friendly Letter:

William   Dear Joey,   Pine Grove, TX 00067

Your friend,   May 3, 20——   208 Valley Drive

    We want you to visit us soon. We will go fishing, have picnics, and ride our motorcycles. It will be a great summer break! Write back when you can.

Friendly Letter

1. Title: _____

_____

_____

_____

2. Title: _____

_____

3. Title: _____

_____

_____

_____

_____

4. Title: _____

_____

5. Title: _____

_____

Notes: _____

Classroom Practice 71

Name:_____ Date:_____

SKILLS AND EDITING

Write the capitalization and punctuation rule numbers for each correction in bold. Use References 11, 13, and 14 on pages 13–14 and 17–19 to look up rule numbers. (Total rule numbers required: 30)

228 Flower Drive

Chicago, IL 00003

March 22, 20—

Dear Grandmother,

Our plane leaves for Tokyo, Japan, on Monday, April 2. This will be an exciting

trip. I wish you could go with us. I'll write again soon.

Love,

Andy

Notes: _____

_____

_____

_____

_____

_____

_____

_____

_____

_____

_____

_____

_____

_____

_____

_____

_____

_____

_____

_____

_____

_____

_____

_____

_____

_____

_____

_____

_____

_____

🏠 Homework 13

Complete the homework assignment on notebook paper. Choose one of the following writing prompts:

1. Write a friendly letter to the author of your favorite book.

2. Pretend you are writing a friendly letter to a pen pal in another state for the first time. You must tell your new pen pal some interesting things about yourself so that he/she can get to know you. Use a social studies book, the library, or the Internet to help you pick the city and state where your imaginary friend lives.

Follow the friendly-letter form. Make up a reasonable name and address. You could research names from the state you choose. Even though this is a pretend pen pal, make sure you always use writing etiquette, or manners. This means you should not write anything that would embarrass your family, teacher, or school.

Note: For a letter-writing assignment in Lesson 7, you should bring an envelope from home. Also, bring the name and address of a friend or family member to whom you will write and mail your friendly letter.

Home Connection

The following activity can be performed at home to enrich language skills and to practice concepts taught.

Family Activity for the Friendly Letter

First, glue the friendly letter below onto cardstock or construction paper. Cut the sections apart at the dotted lines and glue or write the number and the title for each friendly-letter part on the back of the corresponding strip.

Divide into teams. Time each team as members put the pieces of the friendly-letter puzzle together and identify each part. Check the correct answers with the number and title on the back of each piece. The team that completes the puzzle correctly in the shortest time is the winner.

Friendly Letter

Titles: | 1. Heading | 2. Greeting or Salutation | 3. Body | 4. Closing | 5. Signature

---

72 Queens Avenue
Goldberg, OH 00004
June 20, 20——

Dear Uncle Frank,

    Our new colts are wonderful. I can't wait for you to see them. In fact, we've named one of them Frankie after you. I'm looking forward to seeing you in July.

Your nephew,

Thomas

Thomas	5. Signature
Your nephew,	4. Closing
Our new colts are wonderful. I can't wait for you to see them. In fact, we've named one of them Frankie after you. I'm looking forward to seeing you in July.	3. Body
Dear Uncle Frank,	2. Greeting or Salutation
72 Queens Avenue Goldberg, OH 00004 June 20, 20——	1. Heading

Classroom Practice 72

Name: _____ Date: _____

SKILLS AND EDITING

Write the capitalization and punctuation corrections only.
Editing Guide: End Marks: 6   Capitals: 28   Commas: 4

25 kingston road

new york city ny 00004

june 13 20—

dear mom and dad

   i am having a great time aunt sara and i are doing something new every day

we went to the statue of liberty yesterday it was wonderful we are going to the rainbow

chocolate company this afternoon we will spend the day at the atlantic ocean tomorrow

love you

holly

Notes: _____

_____

_____

_____

_____

_____

_____

_____

_____

_____

_____

_____

_____

_____

_____

_____

_____

_____

_____

_____

_____

_____

_____

_____

_____

Chapter 15 Checkup 73

Name:_____ Date:_____

SKILLS AND EDITING

Write the capitalization and punctuation corrections only.
Editing Guide: End Marks: 6   Capitals: 17   Commas: 5   Apostrophes: 1

408 linda lane

springhill ar 00287

october 14 20—

dear joseph

    it was great to hear from you i will send you a picture of james and me riding our

new four-wheeler weve never had as much fun except for the times you were with us

we put a new roof on the barn last week now the horses will have a dry place write soon

your cousin

waylon

Notes: _____

_____

_____

_____

_____

_____

_____

_____

_____

_____

_____

_____

_____

_____

_____

_____

_____

_____

_____

_____

_____

_____

_____

_____

_____

_____

_____

_____

_____

Classroom Practice 74

Name:_____ Date:_____

SKILLS

Use the title and letter parts below to fill in the blanks of the business letter.

TITLE PARTS of a Business Letter:

Closing	**Signature**	**Heading**
Salutation	**Body**	**Inside Address**

SAMPLE PARTS of a Business Letter:

Sincerely yours,   Megan Wells   Wiggins Center   May 13, 20—

                          66 Twin Oaks Avenue   141 Lincoln Street

Dear Sir or Madam: Lewis Springs, IA 00012   Chicago, IL 00060

I am interested in your new math games. I am looking for something to help me with math facts. I am in the third grade. Please send me a catalog.

Business Letter

1. Title: _____

2. Title: _____

3. Title: _____

4. Title: _____

5. Title: _____

6. Title: _____

SHURLEY ENGLISH

Notes: _____

_____

_____

_____

_____

_____

_____

_____

_____

_____

_____

_____

_____

_____

_____

_____

_____

_____

_____

_____

_____

_____

_____

_____

_____

_____

Classroom Practice 75

Name:_____ Date:_____

SKILLS AND EDITING

Write the capitalization and punctuation rule numbers for each correction in bold. Use References 11, 13, and 14 on pages 13–14 and 17–19 to look up rule numbers. (Total rule numbers required: 42)

P. O. Box 58

Tampa, FL 00011

March 21, 20—

Mr. Tony Smith

37 North Ave.

Austin, TX 00099

Dear Mr. Smith:

I am interested in the two-week tour of Mars and Venus. Would you send me

the pamphlets on these planets? I would also like to make flight plans for July 15.

Sincerely yours,

John T. Thomas

Notes: _____

 **14**

Complete this homework assignment on notebook paper.

Write, revise, and edit, a business letter to the Chamber of Commerce in a city you would like to visit. Ask for brochures and information about hotels, restaurants, unique attractions, and local history. Also, use the Internet, library, or telephone directories to find information that would help you. When you get a response, bring the information you receive to school and share it with your teacher and classmates. Use references 176–178 on pages 417–419.

Note: You should bring an envelope from home for a business-letter assignment in Lesson 5.

Home Connection

Family Activity for the Business Letter

First, glue the business letter below onto cardstock or construction paper. Cut the sections apart at the dotted lines and glue or write the number and the title for each business-letter part on the back of the corresponding strip.

Divide into teams. Time each team as members put the pieces of the business-letter puzzle together and identify each part. Check the correct answers with the number and title on the back of each piece. The team that completes the puzzle correctly in the shortest time is the winner.

Business Letter

Titles: | 1. Heading | 2. Inside Address | 3. Salutation | 4. Body | 5. Closing | 6. Signature |

756 Beech Road
Lawton, OK 00016
August 9, 20—

Senator Bill Holt
15 Fifth Avenue
Stillwell, OK 00097

Dear Senator Holt:

   I am glad you are supporting the parks and wildlife in our area. Keep up the good work.

                                        Sincerely yours,

                                        Chris Brown
                                        Chris Brown

---

6. Signature
Chris Brown
Chris Brown

5. Closing
Sincerely yours,

4. Body
I am glad you are supporting the parks and wildlife in our area. Keep up the good work.

3. Salutation
Dear Senator Holt:

2. Inside Address
Senator Bill Holt
15 Fifth Avenue
Stillwell, OK 00097

1. Heading
756 Beech Road
Lawton, OK 00016
August 19, 20—

Classroom Practice 76

Name:_____ Date:_____

SKILLS AND EDITING

Write the capitalization and punctuation corrections only.

Editing Guide: End Marks: 4 Capitals: 30 Commas: 6 Colons: 1 Periods: 7 Apostrophes: 1

p o box 89

oklahoma city ok 00106

june 3 20—

mr j w rockwell

725 north ave

knoxville tn 00021

dear mr rockwell

   i want to enter my dog in your contest his name is jefferson jefferson saved matthew

my little brother from drowning in our neighbors pool i love jefferson very much

sincerely yours

mary alexander

Notes: _____

_____

_____

_____

_____

_____

_____

_____

_____

_____

_____

_____

_____

_____

_____

_____

_____

_____

_____

_____

_____

_____

_____

_____

_____

_____

_____

_____

_____

_____

Chapter 16 Checkup 77

Name:_____ Date:_____

SKILLS AND EDITING

Write the capitalization and punctuation corrections only.
Editing Guide: End Marks: 4   Capitals: 25   Commas: 5   Colons: 1

1213 pine street

harrison mo 00066

august 10 20—

harper music company

4312 slate drive

penney nc 00192

dear sir or madam

　　my sister bought a music box made by your company i would like to buy one

but the store where she bought hers no longer sells them can you tell me where i might

find one thank you for your help

sincerely

sara barnes

Notes: _____

_____

_____

_____

_____

_____

_____

_____

_____

_____

_____

_____

_____

_____

_____

_____

_____

_____

_____

_____

_____

_____

_____

_____

_____

_____

_____

Chapter 17 Writing Evaluation Guide

Name:_____ Date:_____

ROUGH DRAFT CHECK

_____ 1. Did you write your rough draft in pencil?

_____ 2. Did you write the correct headings on the first seven lines of your paper?

_____ 3. Did you use extra wide margins and skip every other line?

_____ 4. Did you write a title at the end of your rough draft?

_____ 5. Did you place your edited rough draft in your Rough Draft folder?

REVISING CHECK

_____ 6. Did you identify the purpose, type of writing, and audience?

_____ 7. Did you check for a topic, topic sentence, and sentences supporting the topic?

_____ 8. Did you check sentences for the right order, and did you combine, rearrange, or delete sentences when necessary?

_____ 9. Did you check for a variety of simple and compound sentences?

_____ 10. Did you check for any left out, repeated, or unnecessary words?

_____ 11. Did you check for the best choice of words by replacing or deleting unclear words?

_____ 12. Did you check the content for interest and creativity?

_____ 13. Did you check the voice to make sure the writing says what you want it to say?

EDITING CHECK

_____ 14. Did you indent each paragraph?

_____ 15. Did you circle each error and write corrections above it?

_____ 16. Did you capitalize the first word and put an end mark at the end of every sentence?

_____ 17. Did you check for all other capitalization mistakes?

_____ 18. Did you check for all punctuation mistakes?
(commas, periods, apostrophes, quotation marks, underlining)

_____ 19. Did you check for misspelled words and for incorrect homonym choices?

_____ 20. Did you check for incorrect spellings of plural and possessive forms?

_____ 21. Did you check for correct construction and punctuation of your sentences?

_____ 22. Did you check for usage mistakes? *(subject/verb agreement, a/an choices, contractions, verb tenses, degrees of adjectives, double negatives)*

_____ 23. Did you put your revised and edited paper in the Rough Draft folder?

FINAL PAPER CHECK

_____ 24. Did you write the final paper in pencil?

_____ 25. Did you center the title on the top line and center your name under the title?

_____ 26. Did you skip a line before starting the writing assignment?

_____ 27. Did you single-space, use wide margins, and write the final paper neatly?

_____ 28. Did you staple your papers in this order: final paper on top, rough draft in the middle, and prewriting map on the bottom? Did you put them in the Final Paper folder?

SHURLEY ENGLISH

Notes: _____

_____

_____

_____

_____

_____

_____

_____

_____

_____

_____

_____

_____

_____

_____

_____

_____

_____

_____

_____

_____

_____

_____

_____

_____

_____

_____

_____

Classroom Practice 78

Name:_____ Date:_____

SKILLS

▶ **Exercise 1:** For each statement, write **O** (opinion) or **F** (fact) in the blank.

_____ 1. Young people are not respectful.

_____ 2. Melinda has five brothers.

_____ 3. A good night's sleep makes you look better.

_____ 4. Illegal drugs aren't good for your health.

_____ 5. Dogs are messy.

_____ 6. I think everyone should own a bicycle.

_____ 7. A bird has feathers and wings.

_____ 8. Dan is the best pitcher on our team.

_____ 9. Ashley seems upset today.

_____ 10. A trout is a type of fish.

▶ **Exercise 2:** Classify each of these sentences in terms of the propaganda technique it contains. **L** (loaded words), **I** (important/famous people), **B** (bandwagon)

_____ 1. Buy a Liberty vehicle. Vince Armstrong drives one, and you should, too!

_____ 2. Our beautiful beagle puppies are a great deal for only $100 each!

_____ 3. Everyone at our school owns a Pocket Pet! Buy yours today at Terry's Toys!

_____ 4. Will's Water Beds help you sleep better. Ahh! For a comfy, cozy snooze, choose Will's.

_____ 5. Most of the ladies will help in the booth at the fair. You probably should, too!

_____ 6. The Mayor of Danville eats at Sam's Seafood. Come to Sam's – where all the big fish are!

SHURLEY ENGLISH

Notes: _____

_____

_____

_____

_____

_____

_____

_____

_____

_____

_____

_____

_____

_____

_____

_____

_____

_____

_____

_____

_____

_____

_____

_____

_____

_____

_____

_____

Classroom Practice 79

Name:_____ Date:_____

SKILLS

▶ **Exercise 1:** Underline the key word(s) in each question. The words *butterflies* and *moths* cannot be used as key words. Scan for the answers in the article in Reference 196. Write only the section number where you will find the answer.

Section:_____ 1. What is one way that butterflies and moths are alike?

Section:_____ 2. What is one way that butterflies and moths are different?

Section:_____ 3. How are the antennae of butterflies and moths different?

Section:_____ 4. What is nectar?

▶ **Exercise 2:** Using Reference 196, write the answers in the blanks below and put the numbers of the sections where the answers were found.

Answer List:

| wings | antennae | long | spread | nectar |
| chubby | short | legs | folded up | slender |

Section:_____ 1. Insects have six _____ and usually have _____.

Section:_____ 2. A butterfly's body is _____ and _____.

Section:_____ 3. Both butterflies and moths have _____ for smelling.

Section:_____ 4. A moth's body is _____ and _____.

Section:_____ 5. Both butterflies and moths drink _____, the sweet liquid in flowers.

Section:_____ 6. Butterflies rest with their wings _____, but moths rest with their wings _____.

▶ **Exercise 3:** Using the article in Reference 196, write the answers in the blanks below and put the number of the section where the answers are found.

Section:_____ 1. Give two ways that butterflies and moths are alike.

_____

_____

_____

_____

_____

Section:_____ 2. Give two ways that butterflies and moths are different.

_____

_____

_____

_____

SHURLEY ENGLISH

Notes: _____

_____

_____

_____

_____

_____

_____

_____

_____

_____

_____

_____

_____

_____

_____

_____

_____

_____

_____

_____

_____

_____

_____

_____

Classroom Practice 80

Name:_____ Date:_____

SKILLS

▶ **Exercise 1:** Copy the notes below into an outline. Use the correct outline form.
(The notes are in correct parallel form.)

NOTES:	OUTLINE:
ways to travel	
introduction	
water travel	
ship	
boat	
raft	
air travel	
airplane	
jet plane	
prop plane	
helicopter	
Land travel	
by car or truck	
by train	
by cycle	
bicycle	
motorcycle	
conclusion	

▶ **Exercise 2:** Place an **X** in front of the items that are parallel.

_____ 1. smooth skin   _____ 3. long legs

_____ 2. slender body   _____ 4. hops and swims

Notes: _____

Chapter 19 Checkup 81

Name:_____ Date:_____

SKILLS

▶ **Exercise 1:** Before each statement, write **O** (opinion) or **F** (fact) in the blank.

_____ 1. Everybody loves babies.

_____ 2. The capital of Japan is Tokyo.

_____ 3. Alaska is a good place to visit.

_____ 4. Scientist are the smartest people in the world.

_____ 5. There are seven days in a week.

▶ **Exercise 2:** Classify each of these sentences in terms of the propaganda technique it contains. **L** (loaded words), **I** (important/famous people), **B** (bandwagon)

_____ 1. KoolMan Ice wears black leather. Be like KoolMan, wear leather. On sale at Murphy's.

_____ 2. Turn your dull porch into a beautiful and peaceful patio room! Call Patio Pros today!

_____ 3. Satisfy your thirst! A fruity lemon-cherry slush from Blinkies — What could be better?

_____ 4. Mom, I need some dangle earrings! Everybody's wearing them.

_____ 5. Everyone will be at the beach today. Why aren't you going?

▶ **Exercise 3:** Put the notes into a two-point outline form. (The notes are in correct parallel form.)

NOTES:	OUTLINE:
eating ice cream	
in a shake	
add milk	
add fruit or candy	
in a sundae	
add chocolate syrup	
add nuts	
add whipped cream	

▶ **Exercise 4:** Place an **X** in front of the items that are parallel.

_____ 1. the backyard   _____ 3. on the sidewalk

_____ 2. on the driveway   _____ 4. in the yard

Notes: _____

_____

_____

_____

_____

_____

_____

_____

_____

_____

_____

_____

_____

_____

_____

_____

_____

_____

_____

_____

_____

_____

_____

_____

_____

_____

_____